The Story of
GEORGE LOVELESS
and the Tolpuddle Martyrs

DR ANDREW NORMAN

HALSGROVE

First published in Great Britain in 2008
Copyright © 2008 Andrew Norman

British Library Cataloguing-in-Publication Data
A CIP record for this title is available from the British Library

ISBN 978 1 84114 838 0

HALSGROVE

Halsgrove House
Lower Moor Way
Tiverton, Devon EX16 6SS
Tel: 01884 243242
Fax: 01884 243325
email: sales@halsgrove.com
website: www.halsgrove.com

Printed and bound by
The Cromwell Press, Trowbridge

Contents

Dedication

In loving memory
of
Arthur Ernest Jordan
and
Christopher Arthur Norman

About the Author

Andrew Norman was born in Newbury, Berkshire, UK in 1943. Having been educated at Thornhill High School, Gwelo, Southern Rhodesia (now Zimbabwe) and St Edmund Hall, Oxford, he qualified in medicine at the Radcliffe Infirmary. He has two children Bridget and Thomas, by his first wife.

From 1972-83, Andrew worked as a general practitioner in Poole, Dorset, before a spinal injury cut short his medical career. He is now an established writer whose published works include biographies of Thomas Hardy, TE Lawrence, Sir Francis Drake, Adolf Hitler, Agatha Christie, and Sir Arthur Conan Doyle. Andrew was remarried to Rachel in 2005.

All Andrew Norman's books are displayed on his website andrew-norman.com

Acknowledgements

I am grateful to the following people and organizations for their help and generosity:

United Kingdom
British Library; Dorchester Methodist Circuit; Dorset County Museum; Dorset History Centre, Dorchester; HM Prison, Dorchester; House of Lords Record Office, London; John Wesley's Chapel, Broadmead, Bristol; Keep Military Museum, Dorchester; London Metropolitan Museum; London Metropolitan University, TUC Library Collections; Meteorological Office; Methodist Archive, John Rylands University Library, Manchester; National Archives, Kew; National Meteorological Office Archive, Exeter, UK; Parliamentary Archives, Houses of Parliament, London; Poole History Centre; Poole Central Library; Portsmouth City Council Library Service, Portsmouth, Hants; Royal Institute of British Architects Trust Ltd; Somerset and Dorset Family History Society, Sherborne; Tolpuddle Martyrs' Museum, Tolpuddle, Dorset; University of Warwick, Modern Records Centre; Wesley Centre, Westminster Institute of Education, Oxford Brookes University, Oxford; West Dorset District Council, Dorchester, Dorset.

Canada
The London Free Press, London, Ontario; London Public Library, London, Ontario; Western Archives, University of Western Ontario, London, Ontario; University of Western Ontario, JJ Talman Regional Collection, London, Ontario.

Australia
Archives Authority of New South Wales, Sydney; Archive Office of Tasmania, Hobart, Tasmania; City State Records Authority of New South Wales, Kingswood, NSW.

Individuals

Geoffrey Anderson; Reverend Paul Arnold; Barry Arnott; Michael J Boggan; Lisa Burke; Margaret Clapperton; Christine Coates; Norman Crocker; Michael Dragffy; Robyn Eastley; Jacqueline Edwards; TG Ellis; Peter Forsaith; Phillippa Francis; Reverend Benny Hazlehurst; Helen Jones; Joan Jordan; Beth King; Donna King; Dr Peter Knockles; Katrina Legg; Judy Lindsay; Keith Loveless; Ian MacGregor; Ann Martin; Arthur McClelland; Jo Miller; Karen Munro-Caple; Phyllis Munro; Nicki Ottavi; Pat Parker; Myra Pearson; Janet Pickering; Annie Pinder; Steven Powrie; Theresa Regnier; Martin Saunders; Jeffrey Spittall; Gary Standfield; Lloyd N Thomas; Alan Ventress; Wendy Waldron; Richard Ward; Audrey Wirdnam.

I am especially grateful, as always, to my dear wife Rachel, whose beloved late father Arthur Jordan, was Dorset County Organiser of the National Union of Agricultural Workers.

God is our guide! from field, from wave,
From plough, from anvil, and from loom;
We come, our country's rights to save,
And speak the tyrant faction's doom:
    We raise the watch-word liberty;
    We will, we will, we will be free!

God is our guide! no swords we draw,
We kindle not war's battle fires;
By reason, union, justice, law,
We claim the birth-right of our sires:
    We raise the watch-word liberty
    We will, we will, we will be free!

George Loveless, 19 March 1834

Preface

In late August 1934, the sleepy Dorset village of Tolpuddle, with its archetypal thatched cottages, farms, and 12th century parish church, suddenly became abuzz with excitement. Celebrations were in hand to commemorate the village's six famous sons: brothers George and James Loveless; Thomas Standfield and his son John; James Hammett, and James Brine. 100 years previously, all had been arrested, tried, and transported to Australia. These men subsequently became known as the Tolpuddle Martyrs.

Tolpuddle, Parish church of St John the Evangelist. Photo: Audrey Wirdnam.

The Trade Union Congress (TUC), which in that year had chosen to hold its annual conference at nearby Weymouth, arranged for various commemorative events to take place in south Dorset, including an opening ceremony in Barrack Square, Dorchester. Tolpuddle marked the occasion with a brass band contest and an international sports meeting. A memorial tablet was placed on the wall of Thomas Standfield's cottage - former meeting place of the Martyrs - and six new memorial cottages, built on the west side of the village with the sponsorship of the TUC to house retired agricultural labourers, were dedicated: one to honour each Martyr. On the, hitherto, unmarked grave of James Hammett in the village churchyard, George Lansbury, leader of the Labour Party in the House of Commons, unveiled a new headstone, inscribed by English sculptor Eric Gill. The Vicar of Tolpuddle the Reverend Henry Gilbert, said a prayer; the event being witnessed by 69 year old William Hammett of Dorchester, the late James Hammett's son.

In 1947, Alderman Gooch, President of the National Union of Agricultural Workers, unveiled a plaque on the wall of Dorchester's County Hall (formerly Shire Hall) to commemorate the Martyrs. Since that time, an annual ceremony has been held in Tolpuddle, traditionally on the 3rd Sunday in July, to mark the event and to pay tribute to these brave, and much wronged men. The ceremony includes the placing of a wreath on the grave of James Hammett, the only Martyr not to have emigrated to Canada.

George Loveless, the acknowledged leader of the Tolpuddle Martyrs, wrote two brief accounts: one of his arrest, imprisonment, and trial; the other, of his experiences in Australia as a transported convict. Apart from this, however, a shroud of mystery hangs over his life, owing to a pact of secrecy which he, and those four of his companions who, like him, emigrated to Canada following their return from Australia, swore to one another. Nevertheless, by painstaking research, not only in the United Kingdom, but also in Canada and Australia, it is now possible to reveal many, hitherto, unpublished details about George Loveless's life. This is the story of how Methodism – for George Loveless was a staunch Methodist – was originally brought to Tolpuddle, and of the intense and violent prejudice which existed against such 'dissenting' religions at that time; of the socio-economic forces which compelled Loveless to establish his Tolpuddle trade union, and of the sly pretext on which the authorities arrested and charged him in 1834. We sense the humiliation of this righteous and God-fearing man as he is marched, unceremoniously, through the streets of Dorchester en route to His Majesty's Prison. We sense the anguish of his family, as he is sent to the dreaded convict settlement of Van Diemen's Land in Australasia. Finally, we learn of his triumph when he, together with his brother James, Thomas and John Standfield, and James Brine makes a new and successful life in Canada.

The quest for George Loveless has been a productive one. A great deal of his background, together with details of his parents, siblings, and family has been unearthed. The names of the members of his Tolpuddle union, and the oath which new members swore on joining it, has been rediscovered amongst papers held in the British Library.

Since Loveless's time, much of the village of Tolpuddle has been rebuilt, and the knowledge of where, exactly, George Loveless and the other Martyrs lived (with the exception of Thomas and John Standfield's abode, which is known), is lost in the mists of time. However, the author has been able, not only to identify the sites on which the Martyrs' cottages stood, but also, to his surprise and delight, to confirm that George Loveless's cottage still exists - as a listed building - although nobody in Tolpuddle, or indeed anywhere else, for that matter, was aware of this fact, prior to the publication of this book.

Finally, thanks to the generosity of Martyr descendants in Canada, Australia, and of course, the United Kingdom, many new and hitherto unpublished facts about the Martyrs together with photographs of them, have come to light. How gratifying it is to know, for example, that George Loveless, who once left Tolpuddle in shackles and chains, had the pleasure, in his later years, of cultivating roses, and making himself a rocking chair.

1

An Arrest

The place is the village of Tolpuddle (population about 350), lying 8 miles or so to the east of Dorchester, county town of Dorsetshire (Dorset) in southern England. The date is 26 February 1797, the thirty-seventh year of the reign of King George III. Thomas Loveless and his wife Dinah, can be seen making their way from their cottage, along the main street, and up Church Hill to the church. In her arms, Dinah is carrying their sixth child George, born 24 days previously on 2 February; he is to be baptised by the Reverend Dr Bernard Hodgson, Vicar of Tolpuddle since 1775. The day is fine and mild, following an overnight frost.[1]

Tolpuddle, Church Hill (West Farm's barns on left). Photo: Dorset County Museum.

In the year 1824, George Loveless, now aged 27 and a 'labourer in husbandry' (cultivator of the land),[2] follows the same path to the church: this time to be married to Elizabeth Snook of the nearby village of Dewlish. Although Loveless is a staunch Methodist – in fact, a qualified preacher in the Methodist Church – he is to be married in Tolpuddle's 12th century Anglican (Church of England) parish church of St John The Evangelist. The ceremony will be performed by the Reverend Thomas Warren (who succeeded the Reverend Hodgson as vicar on the death of the latter in 1805). It is the 26th of December, and again, the day is a mild one, with the occasional shower.[3]

Ten years later, on Monday 24 February 1834, which is two days before his thirty-seventh birthday, George Loveless, in his words, 'arose to go to my usual labour.'[4] He and his wife Elizabeth ('Betsy') now have three children: George (aged 9), Robert (aged 7), and Thomas (aged 5). On this day, the weather is mild, with mist which will persist until the early afternoon when the rain will come.[5] Having had his breakfast, Loveless, 5 foot 5 inches tall, with, 'very dark brown' hair, and, 'dark grey' eyes[6] attires himself in the customary smock-frock (outer, linen garment), boots, and gaiters (covering for the lower leg as far as the knee). He says goodbye to Elizabeth, closes the door and begins walking down the street to the farm which is his place of work.

Loveless has taken but a few steps when he is approached by the constable of the parish, James Brine, who informs him that he has a warrant from the magistrates for the arrest, not only of him, but also for five of his companions and fellow labourers. These are his younger brother James (25, agricultural labourer, married to Sarah, with 2 children and another expected); Thomas Standfield (44, labourer, married to the Loveless's sister Dianne,[7] with 6 children); Thomas Standfield's eldest son John (21, agricultural labourer, single, living with his parents); James Hammett (21, labourer, married to Harriett, with a one-year-old son); James Brine (21, labourer, single, whose mother Catherine, née Parnacott, was the widow of John, a shoemaker, with four younger children to support). James Loveless, like his brother George, is of the Methodist persuasion, as are Thomas and John Standfield. Also like George, James Loveless and Thomas Standfield are Methodist preachers.[8] When George Loveless enquires of Constable Brine as to the contents of the warrant, the latter holds it out to him, saying, 'Take it yourself. You can read it as well as I can.' (In fact, all six men could read and write).

George Loveless had recently created a trade union in Tolpuddle; new members being admitted to it in a ceremony which involved the swearing of a secret oath. According to the warrant now placed before the men by Constable Brine, however, the swearing of such an oath was an illegal act, and this was the basis upon which he and his companions were to be charged. Brine now asks, 'Are you willing to go to the magistrates with me?', to which Loveless replies affirmatively, 'To any place wherever you wish me.' Brine now escorts him and the other five men to Dorchester, the county town. This entailed a journey, on foot, of about 8 miles. Little did he, or any of his companions, know that it would be three, long years before they set foot in Tolpuddle again, by which time they would have travelled half way around the world!

1. Meteorological Office, Exeter, Devon, UK.
2. British Library: *Frampton Papers*. Frampton to Melbourne, 29 March 1834, Ms 41567L Folio 161.
3. Meteorological Office, Exeter, Devon, UK.
4. Loveless, George. *The Victims of Whiggery*, p.7.
5. Meteorological Office, Exeter, Devon, UK (from weather diary kept at Hadspen House, Castle Cary, Somerset.)
6. Dorchester Prison Records, Dorset History Centre, Microfilm R/878.
7. Baptised 'Dianne', signed herself 'Dianna', 'Dinniah' on her tombstone.
8. British Library: *Frampton Papers*. Frampton to Melbourne, 29 March 1834, Ms 41567L Folio 161.

2

Simmering Discontent

The sense of social injustice amongst working people, which had prompted George Loveless to create the Tolpuddle union in 1833, had been present for several years, and in August 1830, it boiled over when riots broke out in Kent, and spread westwards to adjacent counties. The rioters, desperate to be paid a living wage, sent threatening letters, signed by the fictitious and ominously named 'Captain Swing', to local farmers and landowners. Some, then resorted to violence and intimidation. In November 1830, a Whig government under Earl Grey, had taken over office from the previous Tory administration of the Duke of Wellington, and it was to the new Home Secretary Lord Melbourne, that the task of crushing the revolt fell.

In the autumn of 1830, *The Dorset County Chronicle and Somerset Gazette* carried a number of letters, editorials and articles which endorsed the fact that all was not well in the countryside. For example, one which appeared on 25 November, under the heading, 'SIGNS OF THE TIMES', read as follows:

> Sir, - That the 'signs of the times' are such as to occasion in every thinking mind very serious, not to say gloomy, apprehensions, will not be denied, however opinions may differ upon the causes or the remedies of the portentous evils threatened by them.

> The proximate causes of outrage and violence that have from time to time prevailed, and are even now unhappily prevailing in this country, may be traced to actual distress — that is to the inability of an industrious population, to obtain, by their labour, that portion of the comforts and conveniences of life that nature demands, and that every human being is by nature entitled to.

The writer proceeded to declare that one cause of the problem was excessive taxation, which ground down, 'by want and privation,' labourers in agricultural districts to the extent that:

15

...their scanty hard-earned wages doled out to them in part through the degrading medium of parish relief — are at best sufficient only just to keep them from starvation...

(This was a reference to the Speenhamland System - the name deriving from a parish in Berkshire, whose magistrates, in 1795, introduced a sliding scale of relief for labourers, which would be determined according to the current price of bread and the size of the individual labourer's family. Its effect was to give farmers *carte blanche* to pay their workers as little as possible, knowing that the balance would have to be provided out of the rates).

Another cause of distress was, 'the improvements in machinery' which had been made in order to, 'facilitate production and lessen labour.' This had not only caused unemployment, but it had also caused the wages of the employed to be reduced.

The author of the letter believed that the present government was genuinely anxious to, 'ameliorate the condition of the people, and to afford them every possible relief,' but was powerless to do so, given that the public debt (on which annual interest was payable) was a massive £800,000,000.[1]

On the same day, in a leading article aptly entitled, 'The Winter of Discontent', the editor of *The Dorset County Chronicle* referred to some 'immediate problems' which needed to be addressed, given the degree of discontent which was evident all around. The article, however, made the restoration of law and order its sole priority, rather than the welfare of the people.

> The disturbances which are taking place in the neighbouring counties, have assumed a most alarming aspect; and although the reports which are afloat combine a mass of absurd exaggeration... yet the truth, as it is proved, is too alarming to be trifled with. The state of the country is at present one of great disorder; the peasantry, deluded by the efforts of political intriguers, have now excited among them a spirit of discontent, and of hostility towards their landlords; the alarm which exists throughout the south of England, the riots and destruction of property which we hourly hear of, are such as to convince every one that we live in times of an awful character; and as it is the incumbent duty of the magistracy, not only in the disturbed districts, but also in those counties which border them, to adopt every precautionary measure, to strengthen their power by all available means...

16

For the peace of our own county we fear little; the condition of the peasantry generally is better that it is in many other parts, and their masters ever evince a kind and considerate disposition to meet every complaint, which would render any hostile display on the part of the labourers, a crime of still greater magnitude But still it is necessary that precautionary efforts should be made...

It was a source of satisfaction, that only the previous evening, the local magistrates had assembled together at Dorchester's County Hall, where they had sworn in, 'several hundred special constables, to act for the county...' and to, 'assist in preserving the peace of the town.'

There was, however, one item of encouraging news. The newspaper had recently learned that Edward Berkeley Portman, Esq., of Bryanston, had:

>...given orders that every man on his estates shall have 2s [extra] per day, and has determined to reduce his rents to the standard of 1795 — an example worthy of imitation.[2]

Within a year, Portman's attitude would harden considerably, especially towards those who were attempting to create trade unions, as will shortly be seen.

On 2 December 1830, the editor of *The Dorset County Chronicle* indicated that his worst fears had been realised, for the rioting and destruction had now spread to Dorset itself. Said he:

>Some of those disgraceful disturbances, which have, for some time past, alarmed the kingdom, have at length, as we feared, taken place in our own county.[3]

With the Christmas of 1830 approaching, Members of Parliament had now adjourned for the recess. In this season of goodwill to all men (and presumably to women and children also), this was an excellent opportunity, said the editor of *The Dorset County Chronicle*, for Members to visit the various districts which they represented, in order that they might investigate the condition of the labouring classes, and where distress was proved to exist, enquire into its causes, so that, 'the best and most efficient remedies may be devised.'[4]

The 30 December 1830 issue of *The Dorset County Chronicle*, with its customary emphasis on the importance of maintaining law and order, declared that those who had rioted in Hampshire, Wiltshire, and Dorsetshire, were shortly to be brought to trial:

> …and the terror which will have birth in the infliction of summary and severe punishment upon the ringleaders, will be attended with the most beneficial results in stemming the progress of insubordination for the present.

Such measures would:

> …certainly show the peasantry the personal danger which attends the course they have been pursuing, and the futility of any attempt to better their condition by insurrection.

However, it was:

> …much to be feared that, unless some evidence be displayed that the higher classes do in some measure sympathize in the sufferings of their poorer neighbours, and strive to ameliorate the hardships under which the latter have long suffered, the calm will not be of long continuance, but that, when the terror inspired by the Assizes has been diminished by the operation of time, there will come another explosion of the political volcano.

As to the notion that Parliament could:

> …do nothing to relieve the agricultural labourer; that all the causes which have led to the depression of his state are beyond the scope of legislative interference. We deny the assertion, and the able speech of that worthy and patriotic nobleman, Lord WYNFORD [William Draper Best, a former judge, originally a Whig, who had transferred his allegiance to the Tory party], who, in the House of Lords not long since, was replete with facts and arguments to prove that Parliament is in possession of the power to do much towards restoring a right tone amongst those important classes of the community now labouring under distress.

Taxes could be repealed, and the iniquitous and destructive custom of paying workers an inadequate sum for their labour, and making up the deficiency out of the poor rate, must be dispensed with. In the words of Dorset magistrate DO Okeden, Esq., a 'worthy and learned' man, this system had so crushed the labourers' 'pride of independence', that he had been degraded to the position of a 'Parish slave', and was obliged to pass his days in a, 'cheerless endurance of the present, and in sullen recklessness of the future.'[5]

1. *The Dorset County Chronicle*, 25 November 1830.
2. Ibid, 25 November 1830.
3. Ibid, 2 December 1830.
4. Ibid, 30 December 1830.
5. Ibid, 30 December 1830.

3

The Establishment Clamps Down

The 'Special Commission', which had been set up in late November 1830 to try those accused of committing offences against property and people, swung into operation, with the arrival in Dorchester on 12 January 1831 of John Bond, Esq. of Creech Grange, who was High Sheriff of the county. The following afternoon, Bond set out in a carriage on his important mission to 'Piddletown' [or Puddletown], 4 miles distant. On this, he was accompanied by his chaplain the Rev. G Pickard, jun., escorted by a numerous body of javelin men (judges' escorts), and attended by the Under-Sheriff, County Clerk, and other dignitaries. Here, he met up with their Lordships, the judges Mr Baron Vaughan and Mr Justice Alderson. This was an occasion of some spectacle: some 200 special constables of the county having assembled there also, in order to meet their Lordships. The judges having joined Sheriff Bond in his carriage, the party approached Dorchester accompanied by a mounted body of yeomanry. This body comprised, 'most of the respectable farmers' and others, with magistrate James Frampton at its head.

On entering the town - which they reached at about 5 p.m. - their Lordships proceeded straight away to the Shire Hall, which contained both the County Court and the lower Nisi Prius Court (literally, 'unless before', the name dating from times when cases were tried at Westminster, only if they had not previously been tried elsewhere in the country, both the lower Nisi Prius Court and the adjacent higher Crown Court were contained within Dorchester's 17th century Shire Hall, rebuilt in 1797). Here, the Commission was, 'opened in due form.' This show of strength by the judiciary was undoubtedly intended to impress, and instil a certain degree of fear into the population at large.

The following morning, the judges attended divine service at St Peter's church, taken by the Reverend JM Colson, who was also a magistrate. The Reverend G Pickard then preached the sermon, taking Psalm cxxii, v.6 as his text: 'O pray for the peace of Jerusalem: they shall prosper that love thee' – the implication being that those who chose *not* to live in peace would definitely not prosper! The 'Reverend Gentleman' took note of the, 'infidel and revolutionary spirit which is abroad,' whilst at the same time enlarging upon, 'the duties and qualities of a true patriot.'

In the Nisi Prius Court, Mr Baron Vaughan took the chair, with Mr Justice Alderson at his right hand. Also on the bench were three lay commissioners: the Earl Digby, the Earl of Shaftesbury, and CB Wollaston, Esq. The fifty magistrates present included E B Portman, Esq. M.P., and the ubiquitous James Frampton, Esq. The proceeding of the court would give an indication as to the nature of the offences committed, and, in the event of a 'guilty' verdict, the sentences which were considered appropriate to fit the crimes.

James Wilkins aged 22, was charged with, on 23 November 1830, 'feloniously robbing Henry Moyle of certain monies, his property….' Moyle, a land-surveyor, residing at Aldersholt in the parish of Cranborne, stated that on 23 November at about nine o'clock in the evening:

> …as he was taking his tea with his family, he was aroused by violent knocking at his outer door, and as they [this] increased, he went and opened it, and found the prisoner [Wilkins] standing on the outside, nine or ten other men being a few yards off, just outside the front court gate. The prisoner, who had a large stick in his hand said, 'We want money.' I said "I will give you half-a-crown". That, he refused, saying 'that won't do.'

Moyle then offered Wilkins the sum of 5 shillings, to which the latter replied, 'I'll be damned if I don't have more,' and, 'raising his bludgeon, flourished it about, and struck it against the gate with much violence.' At this, Moyle removed from his pocket all the money he had on his person, which was 8s. 6d., and gave it to Wilkins, who then demanded, 'victuals and drink' for himself and for his companions. Moyle:

> …immediately let them have a large quantity of beer, about three or four gallons, and some bread and cheese, the remnants of which they threw down in the road, after they had divided it and eaten and drank. The main body were at this time coming up [approaching], after having burnt a machine [threshing machine, mechanically driven, for separating grain from straw or husks). About half an hour afterwards the mob came back for more beer.

In his defence, Wilkins told the court that he had been in the employ of a Mr Thompson, until the day when he was, 'compelled to join the mob', which he had attempted to dissuade from attacking a corn mill. 'He had also assisted another party, in dispersing the mob....'

Another prisoner, John Read, was indicted for, 'feloniously robbing Mr J. Brewer, of three sovereigns, his monies,' Brewer stating that on 24 November:

> ...a mob had come to his farm, and that in consequence of various threats, he had been induced to give them, first one sovereign, and afterwards some more, fearing that they would do him some injury. The mob had broken several articles, not machines, used for agricultural purposes, and then threatened to kick up a row, if more money was not given to them.

> The prisoner [Reed] in his defence, said that the money had been given to him by a Mr. Brewer, and that he had not asked for any; he farther stated that afterwards as he was returning home, he had seen Lord Salisbury struggling with a man, who had a bar of iron in his hand... [and that] he had ultimately wrested it from the man, and had given it [the bar] to Lord Salisbury.

In the case of both men, Wilkins and Read, the verdict of the court was that they should have, 'a judgment of death recorded against them.'

Joseph Sheppard and George Legg were found guilty of robbing Christopher Morey of 2 shillings in the parish of Buckland Newton. Both were also sentenced to death, as was Henry Spicer, who had stood trial for having robbed John Young of six half-crowns and 5 shillings.

Of eleven men accused of destroying a threshing-machine, two were acquitted; two were sentenced to three month's imprisonment and to be, 'kept to hard labour'; the remaining seven were sentenced to seven years transportation [the removal of the offender to the colonies].

Seven men, charged with robbery, were acquitted for lack of evidence, as were five others who had been charged with robbing Matthew Galpin of one sovereign, and of threatening to destroy a threshing machine. Five men indicted for riotous assembly, and for obtaining money from the Reverend

John Tomkins, Rector of Stower Provost, were acquitted on the grounds that, 'the evidence did not make out [i.e. support] the charge.' Five men were indicted for, 'feloniously breaking a threshing-machine' - the property of W Coward - and found guilty, though with a recommendation from the jury for mercy.[1]

✦ ✦ ✦

In handing down such harsh sentences, there is no doubt that the judges were mindful, not only of the need to make an example, but also of the events which were taking place on the Continent of Europe. Times were perilous, as the editor of *The Dorset County Chronicle* declared:

> The tornado of revolution which sprung up in France [in 1789] is rapidly spreading over almost every other nation. Belgium, Brunswick, Switzerland, and Poland, have already felt its influence — thrones totter and monarchs succumb to its power.
>
> As we stated last week, we are not inimical to the effort-making by the Poles to throw off the Russian yoke which has so long degraded them. The occurrence of this event has induced much speculation in the political world, as to the increased chances and probabilities of a Continental war.
>
> For ourselves, we have no doubt that ere many months are elapsed, the whole of the Continental nations will be involved in a destructive and protracted war. Russia, Prussia, and Austria, the three great northern powers, are already prepared and ready for hostilities.[2]

It has to be said, however, that this was no excuse for ignoring the genuine grievances of men who, in the main, were neither un-patriotic, nor opposed to the monarchy, and whose simple demand was to be paid a living wage.

---

1. *The Dorset County Chronicle*, 13 January, 1831.
2. Ibid, 23 December 1830.

4

George Loveless's Dilemma: How he was Betrayed

So, knowing the fate of those who had dared to complain about their lot in 1830, and to attempt to do something about it, what made George Loveless - by most accounts a man of moderation - so determined to create his Tolpuddle union? Was it worth antagonising the ruling classes once more, with all the attendant dangers which that involved? Was it really worth risking transportation, or even death?

The answer is to be found in *An Important Memorandum on the Subject of the Labouring Classes* (by an anonymous correspondent), published in a London newspaper, and summarised by *The Dorchester County Chronicle* on 23 December 1830. In his *Memorandum*, the question posed by the author was, what was the:

> …*minimum* quantity and quality of food necessary for the support of one able-bodied agricultural labourer in health and strength, to enable such labourer to perform the work usually required of farm-labourers…?

He then proceeded to list the essential provisions etc. required by a single man per week, with the cost of each item in brackets:

Flour for bread at 10d per loaf (3s 4d)
Bacon, 3½ lbs at 9d per lb (2s 7½d)
Butter, 1lb at 1s per lb (1s 0d)
Cheese, 1lb at 8d per lb (8d)
Beer, 7 pots at 3d per pot (or
an adequate quantity of milk) (1s 9d)
Salt (1d)

Added to this was an amount for:
Lodgings, cooking, and firing (firewood and fuel) (1s 6d)
Shoes (8d)

Clothing (2s 0d)
Washing (6d)
Total 14s 1½d

For a married man, the total weekly outgoings were calculated at an
extra 6d – i.e. 14s 7½d

How then, demanded the author of the *Memorandum*, could a farm labourer
provide adequately for himself, and for his family, when the average wage
paid in the western counties was a mere 6s or 7s per week, i.e., a mere half of
what was needed for the bare necessities? True, the labourer's wages were
occasionally supplemented by a payment of 1s 6d to 2s from the poor rates,
but this he regarded as an, 'iniquitous and demoralising system,' which tended
to, 'break down the spirit, and destroy the independence of the peasant.'

In addition, this 'independence' was further undermined by the Laws of
Settlement of 1834, whereby a person was only eligible for parish relief in his
own parish. This meant that a person was handicapped, should he or she
desire to move around in search of work.

The author had made a point: within the previous three weeks of visiting
about thirty cottages inhabited by the poor, he had enquired of each labourer
as to how many times, during the last three weeks, the family had tasted
bacon? The answer was at seven of the cottages, five times; at nine of the
cottages, only two or three times; at the remaining fifteen cottages, not at
all. (It was true, however, that some of the cottagers kept pigs, but for most,
the price of such an animal (10 shillings - 15 shillings) was prohibitive. How
then, could a labourer perform the amount of work required of him, when
he was effectively limited to a diet of bread and potatoes?

The author's opinion was that the remedy was a simple one. 'A little kind
treatment' was required, together with a modest increase in wages. This,
'would silence all discontents, and prevent the labourers from joining in those
associations (i.e. unions), to which they are instigated, no less by the arts of
designing men, than by the real and substantial evils by which they are
oppressed.' In order to achieve this, it was also necessary for the landlord to
lower his rents to the farmer; this would enable the latter not only to advance
the wages of the labourers, but also to employ more of them.[1]

From the above, it is clear that the Dorset labourer could not afford to support himself, nor his wife and family on his inadequate wages, no matter how hard he worked. Having come to the same conclusion, supported by the above facts, George Loveless had decided that the time had come to act.

❖ ❖ ❖

George Loveless, a highly literate person, explained the background to his creation of the Tolpuddle union in late 1833, in an account entitled *The Victims of Whiggery* (a reference to the Whig administration of 1834-1841); a story which begins with a promise made, and is followed by a betrayal:

> In the years 1831-32, the labouring men of the parish of Tolpuddle met with their employers to request an increase in their wages. The result? The parties came to a mutual agreement: the masters promising to pay the men as much for their labour as the other masters in the district.

The men then returned to their work, the meeting having lasted not longer than two hours, with, 'no language of intimidation or threatening [behaviour].' Shortly afterwards, however, they learnt, that whereas in other places in the vicinity the masters were paying their labourers the sum of 10 shillings per week, the men of Tolpuddle were being paid only 9 shillings, which after some months was reduced, even further, to 8 shillings. Said Loveless:

> This caused great dissatisfaction, and all the labouring men in the village, with the exception of two or three invalids, made application to a neighbouring magistrate, namely William Morden [Morton] Pitt, Esq., of Kingston House, and asked his advice; he told us that if the labourers would appoint two or three of their body, and come to the County Hall the following Saturday, he would apprize the chief magistrate [of the Dorchester division], James Frampton, Esq. (whose name I shall not soon forget), and at the same time our employers should be sent for to settle the subject.

At the meeting, at which George Loveless was one of those nominated to appear, the men were told that they must work for what their employers thought fit to pay them, there being in existence, 'no law to compel masters to give any fixed sum of money to their servants.' In vain the men remonstrated that not only had an agreement been made, it had also been witnessed by none other than Tolpuddle's vicar, the Reverend Thomas Warren, who at that time had said of his own accord:

> I am witness between you men and your masters, that if you will go quietly to your work, you shall receive for your labour as much as any men in the district; and if your masters should attempt to run from their word, I will undertake to see you righted, so help me God!

In fact, said Loveless, as soon as Warren, whom he described as 'a hireling parson' (derogatory term for a person who works for hire), was reminded of this, he, 'denied having a knowledge of any such thing.'

Matters now went from bad to worse, for according to Loveless, wages were now reduced to seven shillings per week, and shortly afterwards the employers declared that they intended to lower them to six. Said he:

> We consulted together what had better be done, knowing it was impossible to live honestly on such scanty, means. I had seen at different times accounts of Trade Societies, I mentioned this, and it was resolved to form a friendly society among the labourers, having sufficiently learnt that it would be vain to seek redress either of employers, magistrates, or parsons.

1. *The Dorchester County Chronicle*, 27 December 1830.

5

Trade Unions and The Establishment

The question of the status of trade unions, which had been a vexed one for many years, was, by the year 1834, largely resolved. However, the present status quo would certainly not have been to the liking of Dorset magistrate James Frampton, who was only too well aware of the threat which the power of organised labour posed to the comfortable way of life of the landed classes.

A trade union is defined as, 'a continuous association of workers having for its prime object the maintenance and improvement of their standards of life and labour.'[1] The first, 'definitely working-class political organisation' in England was being known as the 'London Corresponding Society'. This was founded by a group of skilled workmen in 1792; its name deriving from its *modus operandi*, which was to maintain contact with workmen throughout the land by means of pamphlets and letters. Its aims were: the reform of parliament, and the implementation of adult suffrage - the right of all adults to vote in political elections. The society became defunct in 1794, and just in case anyone should have thoughts of reviving it, it was 'finally suppressed by an Act of Parliament in 1799.'[2] Now followed a veritable plethora of parliamentary acts, whose effect was to make the creation of further trade unions quite impossible.

1795: The 'Treason Act' extended the definition of treason to cover, 'writing which had a tendency to incite the population to hatred or contempt of the Crown or Government.'

1795: The 'Seditious Meetings and Assemblies Act' severely restricted the right of persons to meet in public, by declaring that prior to a venue being designated as suitable for a meeting of unionists, or would-be unionists to be held, a licence was first required from the magistrates, who were also given the right to admission to any such meeting, were it to take place.

1798: The 'Newspaper Act' required that all newspapers be registered,

28

and that prior to a newspaper being published, it must first bear a stamp of authority. This, in other words, was censorship.

1797: 'The Mutiny Act' (37 Geo III c.70 – i.e. an Act passed in the 37th year of the reign of King George III) 'imposing the death penalty on anyone convicted of inciting soldiers or sailors to mutiny.'

1797: (37 Geo III c.123) directed at the suppression of the taking of unlawful oaths.

1799: The first 'Combination Act' (39 Geo III c.81) defined trade unions,- 'of every sort and kind criminal [as] conspiracies by statute as well as at common law.'

1799: The 'Unlawful Societies Act' (39 Geo III c.79) which declared as illegal any society which administered an oath which was not required by law. The Act was also concerned with, 'the complete suppression of a number of the leading Radical Societies' of the day (Radicals being supporters of social and political change).

With the coming of the new century, further legislation came thick and fast:

1800: The second 'Combination Act', amended and strengthened the, 'provisions against trade unions which had been enacted in the previous year.'

1801: An Act renewing and expanding the 1795 'Seditious Meetings and Assemblies Act'.

1812: (52 Geo III c.104) strengthening the 'Mutiny Act of 1797.

1817: The 'Treason Act' (57 Geo III c.6) re-creating and making perpetual, with minor modifications, the treason act of 1795.

1817: (57 Geo III c.19) to deal further with seditious meetings and assemblies.

1819: The Third Act (60 Geo III c.4) expedited the administration of justice in the case of 'Radical agitators'.

1819: The Fourth, 'Seditious Meetings Act' (60 Geo III c.6) was largely in essence, a re-enactment of the Act of 1817, 'but in an even more stringent form.' From now on, if a public meeting were to be held, only the local inhabitants of that parish or township were permitted to attend.

1819: The Sixth Act (60 Geo III c.19) extended the heavy stamp duties already levied on newspapers, to other forms of publication, such as pamphlets and printed papers.[3] One effect of the 1819 'Newspaper Act' was to force William Cobbett, English writer and champion of the poor, to raise the price of his publication *Political Register*, in which he championed the cause of Radicalism, from twopence to sixpence.

It should be remembered that these Acts, passed between 1794 and 1819, were a reflection of the climate of the time. For example, in 1811 and 1812, Luddites (named after their leader, Ned Ludd) in northern counties of England, destroyed machinery newly installed in textile factories, on the grounds that such machines, each of which could do the work of several men or women, would inevitably be the cause of unemployment. In 1816, there was rioting in the City of London by followers of the Spencian Society (named after radical land reformer Thomas Spence), whose object was to promote the public ownership of land. In 1819 came the Peterloo Massacre, when a crowd advocating parliamentary reform, who had assembled peacefully in Manchester's St Peter's Fields, were attacked by cavalry and foot soldiers. This resulted in the deaths of eleven people.

The establishment was also concerned with events taking place abroad, particularly in France. In 1789, there had been a revolution in that country. In 1792, France was declared a republic, and in 1793, its king, Louis XVI and his queen, Marie Antoinette, were executed. This was followed by a reign of terror, instituted by the Jacobins (a radical political group). From 1792-9, there were wars between France and neighbouring European states hostile to the Revolution - the so-called French Revolutionary wars. Finally, in 1799, Napoleon Bonaparte came to power as First Consul of a military dictatorship. Having routed the Austrian army in 1800 at the Battle of Marengo, he crowned himself Emperor in 1804. Hostilities between Britain and France in 1803, led Napoleon to make preparations for the invasion of the former country. However, Britain's naval superiority made this impossible. In 1808, Napoleon invaded Spain, and in 1812, Russia. At the Battle of Waterloo in 1815, Napoleon was finally defeated by the Duke of

Wellington, aided by a Prussian force under Field Marshal von Blücher.

In the light of these facts, the powers that be were understandably nervous about the possibility of working people organising themselves and taking over the country.

Had any early trade unionist suffered as a result of this legislation? The answer is yes, for in 1786, five bookbinders had been sentenced to transportation for two years for striking, in order to get their hours of labour reduced from twelve to eleven per day. And at the beginning of the present century, in 1801 (in the case of Rex Versus Moors), trade unionists had been indicted for 'administering a secret oath' to their members.[4]

In 1824/25, an astonishing volte-face took place when the 'Combination Acts' were repealed. This was largely due to the efforts of English Radical reformer Francis Place, a self-educated London tailor, who had helped to engineer the passage of the Reform Act of 1832 (which extended the vote to almost all members of the middle classes, and introduced a uniform £10 franchise - right to vote - to the boroughs). Also to Joseph Hume, son of a Scottish shipmaster, who became Assistant Surgeon in the British East India Company. M.P. for Middlesex in the 1830s, it was he who secured the enquiry which led to the repeal of the Combination Acts.

Despite this, the struggle for would-be trade unionists remained an uphill one, for although organisations of workers were now permitted to engage in collective wage bargaining, their unions were still subject to legal restrictions, and had no legal protection for their funds.

1. Citrine, Walter (Editor). *The Book of the Martyrs of Tolpuddle, 1834-1934*. London, p.239.
2. Ibid, p.238.
3. Ibid, pp. 204-213.
4. W Maitland Walker, *An Impartial Appreciation of the Tolpuddle Martyrs*, in *Proceedings of the Dorset Natural History and Archaeological Society*, vol. LV, p.5. 1934. Dorchester: Friary Press, p.14.

6

The Tolpuddle Union is Born

In the light of these circumstances, George Loveless may be forgiven for believing that trade unions were now perfectly legal entities. After all, were not such organisations now numerous throughout the country? And if others could create unions, then why not he, who had at least one brother who was already a member of such a union? Loveless, therefore, set about his task with relish; tradition having it that he and his would-be fellow trade unionist companions met regularly together on The Green at Tolpuddle, under the sycamore tree (subsequently known as the 'Martyrs' Tree'), to discuss their plans.

Tolpuddle, Martyrs' Tree, circa 1900. Photo: Dorset County Museum.

Loveless's first port of call was his eldest brother John, a flax dresser by trade, who had moved to West Dorset. Said he:

I inquired of a brother to get information how to proceed, and shortly after, two delegates from a Trade Society [the Grand National Consolidated Trades Union – GNCTU - of London, founded, in 1833, by Welsh social and educational reformer Robert Owen] paid us a visit, formed a Friendly Society among the labourers, and gave us directions how to proceed. This was about the latter end of October, 1833.

John responded by sending George a copy of the rules of the Flax Dressers Trade Union of Leeds - to which he, undoubtedly, belonged – together with other information relating to it.[1]

The thorough and professional way in which the rules of the Tolpuddle union were drawn up is an indication of just how assiduous and painstaking George Loveless and his companions were in their new found task. Firstly, it was decreed that the society be called the 'Friendly Society of Labourers' (Friendly Societies, legally recognised since 1797, having originally been created for the purpose of enabling people to make financial provision for themselves in their old age). The Tolpuddle union's rules included the customary provision for the appointment of officers of lodges (meeting places), including 'president, vice-president, secretary, treasurer, conductor, warden, and outside and inside guardians,' who were to be elected at the end of each quarter. In the event, George Loveless was appointed President, and George Romaine from nearby Bere Regis (a fellow Methodist lay preacher), Secretary.

It was also stipulated that, 'meetings were to be held once a fortnight for the transaction of business,' and that, 'there shall be one pass-word' required for admission, 'into all Lodges of this Order', the password, 'to be changed once a quarter.' These meetings would be held at the cottage of Thomas Standfield, George Loveless's fellow Methodist preacher, who was also, like him, a trustee of Tolpuddle's Wesleyan Chapel.

The Grand Lodge of the Union was to be based at Tolpuddle, with further lodges to be established in every parish in the vicinity, together with a local committee, which would ensure, 'regularity in the payment of allowances to families who may be standing out… [i.e. striking].' Following his 'initiation into this Order,' a member was required to pay a joining fee (unstipulated, but in practice, one shilling), following which contributions to the Society were fixed at the sum of twopence per week, but in case of any emergency the Committee would have the power to raise this to any amount which it considered necessary in order to, 'meet the urgency of the case.' No Member would be required to pay contributions during periods of sickness or unemployment.

Now came the crux of the matter. If any Master was to attempt to reduce the wages of workmen who were members of the Order, then those members, 'shall instantly communicate the same to the Corresponding Secretary, in order that they may receive the support of the Grand Lodge.' Meanwhile, they must, 'use their utmost exertions to finish the work they may have in hand, if any, and shall assist each other so that they may all leave the place [of work] together, and with as much promptitude as possible.'

If any Member of the Society, 'renders himself obnoxious to his employers solely on account of taking an active part in the affairs of the Order', and provided that he was otherwise, 'guilty of no violence or insult to his master,' and was:

> ...discharged from his employment solely in consequence thereof, either before or after the turn out [strike], then the whole body of men at that place shall instantly strike, and no member of this society shall be allowed to take work at that place until such member be reinstated in his situation.

If any Member of the Order were to divulge:

> ...any of the secrets, or violate the obligations of the same, his name and a description of his person and crime shall immediately be communicated to all Lodges throughout the Country, and if such person gets work at any place where a Lodge is established, or where men belonging to this Order are working, they shall decline to work with such an individual, shall instantly leave the place, and shall receive the support of the Grand Lodge as if they were turning out against the reduction of wages.

It was emphasised that the object of the Society could never be promoted by any act or acts of violence, which would only serve, 'to injure the cause and destroy the Society itself.' It was also made clear that members were expected to behave in a dignified manner; no obscenity would be tolerated, 'in either songs or toasts,' and, 'no political or religious subjects [were to] be introduced during lodge hours.' No member was permitted, 'to eat, read,

34

sleep, swear, bet wagers, or use any abusive language during Lodge hours.'

Finally, it was stipulated that a box was to be kept, 'wherein shall be deposited the Cash, Books, Regalia &c. of the Lodge. The keys to be kept by the President, Vice, and Wardens.'[2]

By the standards of today, this would appear to be an entirely reasonable document, with the Society's emphasis on non-violence, and concern for its members, particularly in times of extra need, and the maintenance of good behaviour and etiquette.

The local farmers and landowners, however, saw matters in a completely different light. No matter that there were unions already established elsewhere, particularly in London and the North of England, this did not mean that they were acceptable in rural Dorset. No, here they must be strangled at birth. The question was, how to go about it, given the fact that unions were no longer, in themselves, illegal entities.

---

1. British Library: *Frampton Papers*. Frampton to Melbourne, 29 March 1834, Ms. 41567L Folio 161.
2. Ibid, Ms.41567L Folio 141.

7

James Frampton: Tyrant-in-Chief

It was through the efforts, above all, of James Frampton of Moreton House, that George Loveless and his companions found themselves in their present, precarious situation. Magistrate; Lieutenant-Colonel in the Dorset Yeomanry; former High Sheriff of Dorset, and squire of the Dorset village of Moreton, it was Frampton who had been most active in investigating the affairs of the Tolpuddle union. This had proved a most difficult task as the Union, created by George Loveless in the autumn of the year 1833, was, in effect, a secret society.

A letter written by Frampton to Earl Digby, Lord Lieutenant of Dorset, dated 30 January 1834, reveals just how assiduous the former was in pursuing his task; also, that he had been on the trail of the Tolpuddle men for some time:

> I am sorry to inform you that within the last fortnight I have had information that nightly meetings have been held by the agricultural labourers in the parishes of Tolpuddle and Bere Regis [4 miles to the east of Tolpuddle], where societies, or, as I believe they are called, unions, are formed. Where they bind themselves by an oath to certain activity.... I am told... they [prospective union members] are conveyed blindfolded to the [meeting] place and do not see the person who administers the oath...'

> ...I cannot as yet get any information as to the precise nature of the activity to which they are sworn but I am informed they are to strike [from] work whenever ordered by their superiors, and that this is to take place at a time when their labour is most required by the farmers; that they are to demand an increase of wages; that they are bound to some other points which I cannot exactly ascertain.

> There is great difficulty in getting information, but I know the numbers are increasing, and that some persons of Affpuddle, Briantspuddle, and Turnerspuddle [villages adjacent to Tolpuddle] have lately been sworn in. Under these circumstances... we have

thought it our duty to write a letter to the Secretary of State [Home Secretary Lord Melbourne] and make him acquainted generally with what is going on....[1]

On the same day, Frampton wrote to Home Secretary Lord Melbourne as follows:

I am requested by some of the Magistrates acting for the Divisions of Dorchester and Wareham in this County, and who are resident in this vicinity, to represent to your Lordship that they have received information from various quarters (of the authenticity of which they cannot entertain a doubt), that Societies are forming amongst the Agricultural Labourers in parts of these Divisions, in which the labourers are induced to enter into combinations [another name for unions] of a dangerous and alarming kind to which they are bound by oaths administered clandestinely. The information which the Justices have obtained as yet seems to apply to a few Parishes only, and more particularly to the Parish of Tolpuddle in the Division of Dorchester, and [to] Bere Regis in the Division of Wareham; in both of which Parishes nightly meetings have been held.

As no specific proof of the time or place of these meetings or of the individuals forming them, have as yet reached the Justices so as to authorise them to take measures to interrupt the meetings or to notice [take note of] the persons engaged in them; all they have been able to do at present has been to communicate with Trusty persons in the neighbourhood [i.e. informers] and by their means endeavour to trace the proceedings and identify the parties.

Because of the, 'very serious nature of the proceedings and the dangerous consequences which may ensue from their being allowed to spread and to gain strength...,' Frampton felt it only right to appraise Melbourne of the situation, and to request his, 'advice and co-operation in any further measures which it may be thought right to pursue.'[2]

In his reply to Frampton, dated 31 January 1834, and sent by his secretary JM Phillipps, Melbourne revealed that he was of the same mind as Dorset magistrate Frampton, and equally determined to discover how, exactly, the Six Men of Tolpuddle might be successfully prosecuted:

SIR,

I am directed by Viscount Melbourne to acknowledge the receipt of your letter of the 30th instant.

Lord Melbourne thinks the Magistrates have acted wisely in employing trusty persons to endeavour to obtain information regarding the unlawful combinations which they believe to be forming among the labourers.

Lord Melbourne desires me to refer to the 25th section of the 57 Geo. 3rd [III], C.19 [The 'Seditious Meetings and Assemblies Act' of 1817] which in cases of this description has been frequently resorted to with advantage. His Lordship thinks it quite unnecessary to refer to the Statutable provisions relative to the administration of secret oaths.[3]

On this final point, however, his Lordship was to have an abrupt change of mind, as will shortly be seen.

1. British Library: *Frampton Papers*. Frampton to Earl Digby, 30 January 1834, Ms 41567L Folio 123.
2. Ibid, 30 January 1834, Ms. 41567L Folio 121.
3. Ibid, 31 January 1834, Ms. 41567L Folio 125.

8

Prison

From the day on which George Loveless and his five companions, including his brother James, were arrested - 24 February 1834 - time began to run out; their trial would shortly begin. The same was true for Magistrate James Frampton, who was tireless in his efforts to find incriminating evidence against them.

Dorchester, High West Street, circa 1860 (County Hall near right).
Photo: Dorset County Museum.

The party having arrived at Dorchester, Constable Brine escorted the six men to Wollaston House - home of Mr Charlton B Wollaston, Chairman of the Quarter Sessions and Recorder of Dorset. Also present were Magistrate James Frampton (Senior Magistrate of the Dorchester Division and Wollaston's half-brother), and Edward Legg, a labourer, who was also a member of the union. The men were now asked several questions; to which the somewhat bemused Loveless answered by saying, 'We are not aware that we have violated any law; if so, we must be amenable, I suppose, to that law.' Legg was now asked to identify the men on oath, which he did. Then, without further ado, the six men, in what must have been a painful and humiliating experience, were marched through the streets of Dorchester to His Majesty's (King William IV's) Prison - a sombre and intimidating edifice, situated in the very heart of the town - where they would remain until the next assizes (periodical sittings of judges on circuit, with jury).

Dorchester, His Majesty's Prison, 1856. Photo: Dorset County Museum.

Was George Loveless surprised by this sudden turn of events? Perhaps not entirely, because only three days previously, cautionary placards had been, in his words:

> …posted up at the most conspicuous places [including at Tolpuddle], purporting to be cautions from the magistrates, threatening to punish with seven years transportation any man who should join the [trade] union. This was the first time that I heard of any law being in existence to forbid such societies. I met with a copy, read it, and put it into my pocket.

What Loveless omitted to mention, perhaps because he did not realise their full significance, were the additional words on the 'Caution' to the effect

40

that, 'Any person who shall administer, or be present at, or consenting to the administering or taking [of] any illegal oath… will become Guilty of Felony.'[1] The mention of oath-taking in the 'Caution' also suggests, that even though Melbourne, in his letter to Frampton of 31 January 1834, did not see this as an important factor in the case, his view was not shared by the local magistrates of Dorset, who had posted up the 'Cautions'.

A description of the prison, which was run by a keeper (governor), Robert W Andrews, assisted by two turnkeys (gaolers), is contained in *The History and Antiquities of the County of Dorset* by the Reverend John Hutchins:

> In this building, are united The County Gaol [place of detention], Penitentiary House [reformatory prison], and House of Correction [punishment]. It stands on an eminence, on the north side of the town, on a piece of ground still called the Castle, and which was formerly the site of a building of that description, at the foot of which flows the River Frome. It is bounded by a wall, about 20 feet high… which, from the turnkey's lodge, situate(d) at the north side of it, completely surrounds the whole of the buildings, courts (courtyards) &c., &c.

Hutchins also refers to Mr Blackburn, the, 'eminent surveyor and architect' of the prison, who was, 'a friend of Howard the philanthropist.' This was a reference to Thomas Howard, the great prison reformer (who had campaigned vigorously for the passing of the General Prison Act of 1791, which stipulated that prisons should be subject to regular inspection), with whom Blackburn worked hand in hand. Hutchins also states that work on the prison was commenced in 1789, and that it was completed in 1795 at a cost of £16,179.10s.6d.[2]

Passing through the prison's entrance lodge was a daunting experience in itself, for, as Loveless and his companions would have been only too well aware, it was on its flat, copper-covered roof, that executions took place: the site being chosen deliberately, in order that the public could witness the event from without, just as the prisoners could witness it from within. The six men would also have been aware of the ever present hangman, whose cottage was situated at the foot of the prison, on the opposite side of the River Frome.

The men now found themselves in the Keeper's Court (yard), facing the central block where the Keeper had his apartments. Above them was the chapel, with adjoining cells for those prisoners who had been condemned to death, and above this were windowless cells for refractory prisoners. There were eighty-eight cells in all, contained in four rectangular, three-storey blocks; each connected to the central one by an iron bridge.

Male prisoners, female prisoners, and debtors, were segregated from each other, each having their own 'Airing Grounds' (courtyards where fresh air and exercise were taken). Other categories of prisoner included: Kings Evidence (criminals giving evidence for the Crown against their accomplices); Misdemeanours; Vagrants; Idle Apprentices; Servants for Breach of Contract; Males and Females for Bastardy (having children out of wedlock); Idle or Disorderly Women.

Prisoners were required to work: the men at such crafts as carpentry, weaving, tailoring, shoemaking; the women at spinning, knitting, shirt-making, and hat-lining. Even though George Loveless and his companions were imprisoned here for only a few days, it is quite likely that some meaningful work was assigned to them during their stay. Hot baths were provided, and there was also provision 'for baking [i.e. sterilising] verminous clothing.' There was also an infirmary, attended by a surgeon whose duties included making a quarterly report.

Said Loveless:

> As soon as we got within the prison doors, our clothes were stripped off and searched, and in my pocket was found a copy of the above placard [i.e. the cautionary placard mentioned above], posted in Tolpuddle by the magistrates for all to see], a note from a friend, and a small key. After our heads were shorn, we were locked up together in a room, where we remained day and night, till the following Saturday, when we were called before a bench of magistrates in another part of the prison. Legg again swore to us [i.e. made a sworn statement about the men], differing [which differed] considerably from the first statement. We were then fully committed to take our trial at the next assizes.

> Directly after we were put back [locked up again], a Mr. Young, an attorney employed on our behalf, called me into the conversation room, and, among other things, inquired if I would promise the magistrates to have no more to do with the Union [and] if [so] they

would let me go home to my wife and family. I said, 'I do not understand you.' "Why" said he, "give them information concerning the Union, who else belongs to it, and promise you will have no more to do with it." 'Do you mean to say I am to betray my companions?' "That is just it," said he. 'No; I would rather undergo any punishment.' [Said Loveless.]

For George Loveless, his brother James, and their four companions, the nightmare had begun.[3]

George Loveless gives the date of his arrest as 24 February – a Monday - and states that, 'on the same day' he was sent to the, 'high jail'. However, the Dorchester Prison Records give the date of the committal and admission to that institution of the six men as being 25 February.[4]

The prison chaplain was the Reverend Dacre Clemetson, whose duty it was, 'to preach once in the week and to conduct prayers twice a week and organise a daily reading of The New Testament by one of the prisoners.' Also to, 'visit and converse with the prisoners in private as to the state of their minds, and give spiritual advice,'[5] though it is doubtful whether he would have told George Loveless, a Methodist preacher, (or any of his Methodist companions, for that matter) anything that the latter did not know already.

When Clemetson visited the six men, he upbraided and taunted them with being, 'discontented and idle, and wishing to ruin our masters.' George Loveless denied that this was the case. The chaplain then assured them that they were, in his opinion, 'better off' than their masters. How could this be, asked Loveless, when those masters could evidently afford to maintain large numbers of horses, 'for no other purpose than to chase the hare and the fox?' The chaplain then became more conciliatory, asking Loveless what more might be done to, 'increase the comfort of the labourer.' When Loveless expressed the opinion that, 'gentlemen wearing the clerical livery… [such as his present visitor] might do with a little less salary,' Clemetson lost his patience. 'I hope the Court will favour you,' he said sternly, 'but I think they will not; for I believe they mean to make an example of you.'[6]

As Frampton combed the Dorset countryside in search of evidence, the Six Men of Tolpuddle languished in prison, where George Loveless's health began to suffer on account of the insanitary conditions which he encountered within its walls. Said he:

> I had never seen the inside of a jail before, but now I began to feel it
> — disagreeable company, close confinement, bad bread, and what is
> worse, hard and cold lodging, a small straw bed on the flags
> [flagstoned floor], or else an iron bedstead. 'And this', said I to my
> companions, 'is our fare for striving to live honest.'

1. *Tolpuddle: An Historical Account through the Eyes of George Loveless*, p.17.
2. Hutchins, Reverend John. *The History and Antiquities of the County of Dorset*, p.372.
3. Loveless, George. *The Victims of Whiggery*, p.8 From his statement, 'The same day we were sent to the high jail, where we continued until the assizes,' George Loveless appears to differentiate between a 'prison', and the 'high jail', so perhaps 'high jail' referred to a particular part of His Majesty's Prison, there being only one prison in Dorchester at that time.
4. Dorchester Prison Records, Dorset History Centre, Microfilm R/878.
5. Weinstock, Miss MB. *Dorchester Model Prison, 1791-1816* (in *Proceedings of the Dorset Natural History and Archaeological Society for 1956, volume 78*, pp.100,108,109.)
6. George Loveless, op.cit., p.8

9

The Tolpuddle Union: Further Details Emerge

On 1 March 1834, Dorset magistrate, James Frampton, wrote to Home Secretary Lord Melbourne once again on the subject of the, 'unlawful combinations which were entered into by the Agricultural Labourers in several Parishes in this County....' He was pleased to say that he had, finally:

> ...obtained sufficient information on Oath against some of the persons, who appear to be the leaders of this Society in one of the Parishes [i.e. Tolpuddle], to enable me to commit six of them for trial at the next assizes...

He hoped that this action on his part:

> ...may put some check to the proceedings; but I am sorry to say the nightly meetings are carried on much more openly than they were at first. The numbers have increased of late to a great degree. The Societies are extending rapidly into Parishes which had not hitherto been infected by them — and there is reason to believe that, in some cases, these Unions are organised by Strangers who come down as emissaries for that purpose.

It was his opinion that the meetings would:

> ...continue to increase, to an extent which will be truly alarming, unless your Lordship should think proper to recommend the issuing some Proclamation against such Societies, or offer some reward for the discovery of the offenders or take such other steps as your Lordship may think most advisable, in order to convince the people that the endeavours of the Justices to put a stop to such proceedings will be sanctioned by the support and assistance of His Majesty's Government which at this moment would come with very great effect.

Since the creation of the unions, the labourers were, 'becoming very remarkably restless and unsettled...,' their manners having, 'undergone a considerable change.' It was his wish, said Frampton, that measures be adopted, 'with as little delay as possible, which may restore their [the labourers'] minds to their usual state of quietness and order.'[1] Frampton's own mind, it has to be said, was in a state of near panic!

On 3 March 1834, Melbourne asked Frampton to send, at his earliest convenience, copies of the 'Depositions' [allegations and sworn testimonies], which he had prepared, prior to committing the six men for trial at the forthcoming assizes; also with a statement containing, 'all the Information and Evidence which you have obtained respecting the Societies and their Nightly meetings.'[2] On 5 March 1834, Frampton duly obliged. He also forwarded to Lord Melbourne, 'a copy of a letter signed George Romane [Romaine], secretary [of the Tolpuddle union], which was found in the pocket of George Loveless when he was committed to gaol,' and, 'a copy of the Rules of the Society,' which bore the date November 1833. Frampton also sent His Lordship several items discovered in the box which George Loveless kept at his home, soon after his arrest. It had been entrusted to Loveless by the union, and contained its papers, cash, and official regalia.

These items were, firstly, a copy of the oath, 'known to be administered to some, and believed to be administered to all the branches of the Union,' which read as follows:

> I do before Almighty God and this Loyal Lodge most solemnly swear that I will not work with any illegal man or men, but will do my best for the support of wages, and most solemnly swear to keep inviolate all the secrets of this Order, nor will I ever consent to have any money for any purpose but for the use of the Lodge and the support of the trade; nor will I write or cause to be wrote, print, mark, either on stone, marble, brass, paper, or sand, anything connected with this Order, so help me God, and keep me steadfast in this my present obligation. And I further promise to do my best to bring all legal men that I am connected with into this Order; and if I ever reveal any of the rules, may what is before me plunge my soul into Eternity. And may I be disgraced in every Lodge in the kingdom.[3]

This document, which was to be of crucial importance to the prosecution in the forthcoming trial of the Six Men of Tolpuddle, also stated that, 'A person stands in front of the party to whom the oath is administered holding a drawn sword with the point towards his breast.'[4]

Secondly there was a copy of a printed paper headed, *'Flax and Hemp Trade of Great Britain'* (which related to the Flax Dressers Trade Union of Leeds, and had been obtained for George by his eldest brother John). Frampton observed that this document had George Loveless's name written on its reverse side.[5]

Thirdly, 'a List of Names, etc' (i.e. of the Tolpuddle Union's members), made for interesting reading. Exactly fifty names were recorded, including, of course, those of George and James Loveless and their four companions: all presently languishing in a prison cell. In addition to agricultural labourers, many other occupations were represented, for example: William Bartlett, carpenter; George Spicer, dairyman; William Hammett, bricklayer. There was also a pauper Richard Riggs, besides whose name were written the words 'No work' (i.e. he was currently unemployed, and therefore was exempted from the payment of union dues).[6] The three John Lovelesses who were listed as members were probably distant relations (George's eldest brother John having previously moved to West Dorset). Likewise, a Stephen Loveless; another James Loveless, and an Edward Loveless. There were also two Thomas Standfields: the second, presumably, being John's brother (born 1814). Also John Hammett, brother of James (also born 1814), and a William Hammett. Alongside each entry was written the annual fee of 1 shilling, and the monthly fee of fourpence. Most significant were the entries for Edward Legg (joined 14 December 1833), and for John Lock (joined 16 November 1833), both of whom would shortly give evidence against the six men in court.[7]

Frampton now made a most important point, declaring to Melbourne that he and his fellow magistrates were acutely aware of, 'the distinction between meetings held merely for settling the price of labour, and those where oaths are administered....' He and his fellow magistrates had therefore, 'published a Caution in several of the Divisions in hopes of explaining to them [the would-be trade unionists] what was illegal....' Furthermore, he took the liberty of enclosing a copy of this 'Caution' for His Lordship's kind perusal. Couched in the familiar long-winded legal jargon of the day, it read as follows:

CAUTION

WHEREAS it has been represented to us from several quarters that mischievous and designing persons have been for some time past endeavouring to induce, and have induced, many Labourers in various Parishes in this County to attend Meetings, and to enter into Illegal Societies or Unions, to which they bind themselves by unlawful oaths,

47

administered secretly by Persons concealed, who artfully deceive the ignorant and unwary – We, the undersigned Justices think it our duty to give this PUBLIC NOTICE and CAUTION, that all Persons may know the danger they incur by entering into such Societies.

Any Person who shall become a Member of such a Society, or take any Oath, or assent to any Test or Declaration not authorised by Law - Any Person who shall administer, or be present at, or consenting to the administering or taking any Unlawful Oath, or who shall cause such Oath to be administered, although not actually present at the time — Any Person who shall not reveal or discover any Illegal Oath which may have been administered, or any Illegal Act done or to be done - Any Person who shall Induce, or endeavour to persuade any other Person to become a Member of such Societies, will become

GUILTY OF FELONY,
and be liable to be
Transported for Seven Years.

Any Person who shall be compelled to take such an Oath, unless he shall declare the same within four days, together with the whole of what he shall know touching the same, will be liable to the same Penalty.

Any Person who shall directly or indirectly maintain correspondence or intercourse with such Society, will be deemed Guilty of an Unlawful Combination and Confederacy, and on Conviction before one Justice, on the oath of one Witness, be liable to a Penalty of Twenty Pounds, or to be committed to the Common Gaol or Home of Correction for Three Calendar Months; or if proceeded against by Indictment, may be convicted of Felony, and be Transported for Seven Years.

Any Person who shall knowingly permit any Meeting of any such Society to be held in any House, Building, or other place, shall for the first offence be liable to the penalty of Five Pounds: and for every other offence committed after conviction, be deemed Guilty of such Unlawful Combination and Confederacy, and on conviction before one Justice, on the oath of one witness, be liable to a penalty of Twenty Pounds, or to commitment to the Common Gaol or House of Correction, for Three Calendar Months; or if proceeded against by Indictment may be

Convicted of Felony,
and Transported for SEVEN YEARS.

C.B.WOLLASTON.
JAMES FRAMPTON.
WILLIAM ENGLAND.
THOMAS DADE.
JOHN MORTON COLSON.
HENRY FRAMPTON.
RICHARD TUCKER STEWARD.
WILLIAM R. CHURCHILL.
AUGUSTUS FOSTER.

County of Dorset, Dorchester Division, February 22nd 1833.[8]

This then, was the 'Caution' which, according to George Loveless, had been posted up in Tolpuddle on 21 February 1834, only 4 days prior to the arrest of himself and his five companions - the one which he had managed to obtain a copy of, read, and place in his pocket. (The 'Caution' was also printed by *The Dorset County Chronicle* on 6 March 1834.) It had appeared too late for him to act upon its contents, even if he had desired to do so, and in any event, the Tolpuddle union had been swearing in its members since the autumn of the previous year.

The magistrates whose names appeared on the 'Caution' are worthy of note, for this was something of a family affair, there being a degree of nepotism in the proceedings. James Frampton was, of course, the presiding magistrate of the Dorchester Division. CB Wollaston, Chairman of the Quarter Sessions and Recorder of Dorchester, was Frampton's half-brother, and Henry Frampton was James Frampton's son. As to the remainder; William England was a vicar of the Church of England, as was John Morton Colson.

1. British Library: *Frampton Papers*. Frampton to Melbourne, 1 March 1834, Ms. 41567L Folio 130.
2. JM Phillipps to Frampton, 3 March 1834, quoted in Citrine, Walter (Editor). *The Book of the Martyrs of Tolpuddle, 1834-1934*. London, p.164.
3.British Library, op.cit., Frampton to Melbourne, Ms. 514567L Folio 179.
4. British Library, op.cit., Frampton to Melbourne, 5 March 1834, Ms. 41567L Folio 179.
5. British Library, op.cit., Frampton to Melbourne, Ms. 41567L Folio 141.
6. Census, Tolpuddle, 1841.
7. British Library, op.cit., Frampton to Melbourne, Ms. 41567L Folio 141.
8. British Library, op.cit., Frampton to Melbourne, 5 March 1834, Ms. 41567L Folio 141.

10

The Trap is Sprung

In his letter of 5 March 1834, Frampton told Melbourne that for some long time the local justices had known:

> …that nightly meetings have been held (I believe twice a week) in the house of this George Romane [Romaine, secretary of the Tolpuddle union], who I am told is a Methodist Preacher, as are also the two Lovelesses, but his house is situated on a very wild heath….

However, although Frampton had every reason to believe that groups of twenty to thirty people at a time were passing through Bere Regis, together with villagers from other parts, en route to Romaine's house for the purpose of attending meetings, the house itself was:

> …so surrounded by persons on the watch [lookout] that it has been impossible for us to send anybody to procure evidence of what is going on within it. Of late we are told the meetings have been removed from the house of George Romane, to the house of a man by the name of Day, who resides in a cottage of his own near to that of Romane.

> The Persons who attend these meetings have become much more bold of late and instead of going secretly and quietly, go together in bodies talking loudly without restraint, and I am told that on the night of Tuesday, February 25th, an extraordinary meeting was called together on Bere Heath [to which members were summoned] by the Sound of a Horn.

Frampton informed His Lordship that meetings had also taken place in the Parish of Winfrith. He was also able to furnish Melbourne with evidence relating to how the unionists managed to communicate with one another. A 'paper' had come into his possession, a copy of which he enclosed:

> …which was delivered by some person unknown to a carter, who

happened to pass thro' Bere [Regis] on his way to Haselbury (a distant Parish in the Vale of Blackmore) in which he resided, and which the carter was desired to deliver to any working people there...

In fact, it was Frampton's opinion that, 'much encouragement' had been given to local unions:

...by communications from Strangers who have passed thro' the Villages at different times, and who appear to have districts allotted to them, and one great object of these Strangers and of the leaders of the Society seems to be to instil into the minds of the Labourers that these meetings are not illegal and that the Justices have no authority to put a stop to them.[1]

On 6 March 1834 Frampton received a reply from Melbourne's secretary, declaring that His Lordship:

...cannot entertain any doubt that you have acted properly in committing for Trial these individuals, who are affected by the evidence which you have transmitted...

and assuring Frampton that His Majesty's servants would give the matter their, 'most serious attention.'[2]

Frampton was by no means alone in his desire to hunt down and destroy the would-be trade unionists. Local landowner and magistrate E B Portman, for example, on hearing that the six Tolpuddle men had been committed for trial, made his views known to Frampton in no uncertain terms:

I hope you have a complete case for conviction as that will be very important. I find in many parishes that the labourers requested to sign the Church Petitions (where the names of members of the Anglican Church were recorded, those who failed to sign the petition being labelled as 'Dissenters') have declined doing so until they were assured 'that such signature was not against the Unions....' ...Do you mean to proceed at the next assizes? ...it seems to be desirable to expedite the blow and allow it to come from the Judges if possible at once.'[3]

For the six imprisoned men from Tolpuddle, this sounded ominous indeed - Portman's letter implying that he reviled trade unionists just as virulently as he reviled Dissenters (such as Methodists), a view widely shared, no doubt, by the Establishment as a whole.

As time went by, Melbourne came round to the notion, which Frampton had hinted at right from the beginning, that the taking of 'illegal oaths' was a significant factor in the equation. As for Frampton, however, although he was a magistrate in his own right, his knowledge of the finer points of the law was insufficient for him to be able to identify exactly which legal statute would be appropriate for a successful prosecution of this particular case. What he and his fellow magistrates did know, was that their difficulty in supressing the trade unions was, 'considerably increased by the protection afforded [to them] by the statute of the 6th Geo.IV. c.129, S. 4 & 5' (i.e. the Act of 1824/25 by which the Combination Laws of 1799 were repealed, and trade unions effectively legalised).[4]

Now, it was Melbourne's turn to come to the rescue. Having expressed, in a letter to Frampton dated 10 March 1834 his, 'entire approbation' of the course which the latter had pursued,[5] His Lordship now sought the advice of the Law Officers of the Crown. He apprised them of the rapid spread of the trade unions, 'in various parts of the Kingdom', and of how, 'At the meetings of these Societies, secret oaths not to divulge or make known the proceedings of the meeting are administered.' He then requested that the Law Officers, in turn, raise the following questions at the highest level:

> I am directed by Viscount Melbourne to desire you will submit this statement to the Attorney [-General, Sir William Hoare] and Solicitor-General [Sir John Campbell], and after referring them to the Act, 6 Geo.III, c.129, S.4 and 5, 'An Act for repeal of laws relating to the combination of workmen and to make other provisions in lieu thereof.' [This appears to be a mistake, in that the Combination Acts were repealed in the years 1824/25] — also to Statute 57 Geo.III, c.19, Sec.25, 'An Act [of 1817] for the more effectual preventing [of] Seditious Meetings and Assemblies,' and to the Statutes relating to illegal oaths, request they will take the same into their consideration and report their opinion:—

> 1st. — Whether the Societies above described (independently of the administering of secret oaths) are within the 25th Section of 57 Geo.III, c.19, and whether the members of such Societies are punishable under the provisions of that Act or the Act referred to therein.

2nd. — Whether the Societies above described in which are administered secret and illegal oaths are illegal, and how the Societies or the members thereof may be proceeded against.[6]

Finally, the law officers of the Crown came up with an even more ingenious solution to Lord Melbourne's problem, when they recommended to him that it would be infinitely more advantageous to his case, were he to utilise yet another Act, albeit one which was somewhat archaic. Thirty seven years previously, in the year 1797, there had been mutiny in the Royal Navy, at Spithead (Eastern part of the Channel between the English mainland and the Isle of Wight), and at the Nore (naval dockyard at Sheerness on the Isle of Sheppey in Kent, in the estuary of the River Thames), as a consequence of which, an Act was passed (37 Geo.III, c.123 – the so-called and previously mentioned 'Mutiny Act'), which was described as: 'An Act for More Effectually Preventing the Administering or Taking of Unlawful Oaths:

WHEREAS divers [sundry] wicked and evil-disposed Persons have of late attempted to seduce Persons serving in His Majesty's Forces by Sea and Land, and others of His Majesty's Subjects, from their Duty and Allegiance to His Majesty, and to incite them to Acts of Mutiny and Sedition, and have endeavoured to give Effect to their wicked and traitorous Proceedings, by imposing upon the Persons whom they have attempted to seduce the pretended Obligation of Oaths unlawfully administered: Be it enacted by the King's most Excellent Majesty, by and with the Advice and Consent of the Lords Spiritual and Temporal, and Commons, in this present Parliament assembled, and by the Authority of the same, That any Person or Persons who shall, in any Manner or Form whatsoever, administer, or cause to be administered, or be aiding or assisting at, or present at and consenting to, the administering or taking of any Oath or Engagement, purporting or intended to bind the Person taking the same to engage in any mutinous or seditious Purpose; or to disturb the publick Peace; or to be of any Association, Society, or Confederacy, formed for any such Purpose; or to obey the Orders or Commands of any Committee or Body of Men not lawfully constituted; or of any Leader or Commander, or other Person not having Authority by Law for that Purpose; or not to inform or give Evidence against any Associate, Confederate, or other Person; or not to reveal or discover any unlawful Combination or Confederacy; or not to reveal or discover any illegal Act done or to be done; or not to reveal or discover any illegal Oath or Engagement which may have been administered or tendered to or taken by such Person or Persons, or to or by any other Person or Persons, or the Import of any such Oath or Engagement; shall, on Conviction thereof by due Course of Law, be adjudged guilty of Felony, and may be transported for any Term of Years not exceeding Seven Years; and every Person who shall take any such Oath or Engagement, not being compelled thereto, shall, on Conviction thereof by due Course of Law, be adjudged guilty of Felony, and may be transported for any Term of Years not exceeding Seven Years.

Here then, was the answer in a nutshell: a 37-year old Act, which had originally been designed to be applied to personnel serving in His Majesty King George III's armed forces, but which, fortunately for Frampton and Lord Melbourne, contained the added words, 'and others of His Majesty's subjects.'

And yet it is arguable whether even this Act had been infringed by the Six Men of Tolpuddle, given that in no way could they be accused of stirring up mutiny and sedition, and, equally, in no way could their union be described as being an, 'unlawful combination or confederacy.' Not only that, there were by 1834 (in addition to Robert Owen's Grand National Consolidated Trades Union, from which the Tolpuddle men had sought advice) scores of trade unions already in existence, particularly in the north of England. Examples being: the silk weavers, gardeners, shipwrights, joiners, cordwainers, journeymen, tailors, coach painters, trimmers, and brush makers; all of whom admitted new members using an initiation ceremony similar to the one used by the Tolpuddle union.

English writer and champion of the poor, William Cobbett (1763-1835), had declared that in England, agricultural labourers endured less freedom and greater hardships than the negro slaves of America, whom he had seen at first hand. It was, therefore, ironic that the Whig government, which only two years previously had officially abolished slavery throughout the British Empire, was now in the process of persecuting people who were living in conditions of virtual slavery in their very own country!

Frampton's investigations were now complete, and with Home Secretary Melbourne's blessing, he was now in a position to proceed. Meanwhile, said George Loveless:

On the 15th of March, we were taken [from His Majesty's Prison] to the County [Shire] Hall to await our trial. As soon as we arrived we were ushered down some steps into a miserable dungeon, opened but twice a year, with only a glimmering light; and to make it more disagreeable, some wet and green brushwood was served for firing. The smoke of this place, together with its natural dampness, amounted to nearly suffocation; and in this most dreadful situation we passed three whole days.[7]

1. British Library: *Frampton Papers*. Frampton to Melbourne, 5 March 1834, Ms. 41567L Folio 141.
2. Ibid, JM Phillipps to Frampton, 6 March 1834, Ms. 41567L Folio 143.
3. Ibid, EB Portman to Frampton, 7 March 1834, Ms.41567L Folio 148.
4. Ibid, Frampton to Melbourne, 5 March 1834, Ms. 41567L Folio 141.
5. Ibid, JM Phillipps to Frampton, 10 March 1834, quoted in Citrine, Walter (Editor), *The Book of the Martyrs of Tolpuddle, 1834-1934*, p.177.
6. British Library, op.cit., JM Phillipps to Secretary to the Law Officers of the Crown, 10 March 1834, quoted in Padden, Graham (Compiler), *Tolpuddle: An Historical Account through the Eyes of George Loveless*, p.21.
7. Loveless, George. *The Victims of Whiggery*. London, p.8.

11

Arrival of the Justices:
the Indictment

The pomp and pageantry of the 1834 Dorset Lent Assizes was reminiscent of that of the aforementioned Special Commission of January 1831, and presumably, of all other assizes and special commissions held in the county of Dorset before or since (assizes having been held since the reign of King Henry II, 1154-1189). At that time, the country was divided into circuits: each covering several adjoining counties; Dorchester being part of the Western Circuit.

It was Friday, 14 March 1834, when the Honourable Mr Baron Williams arrived in Dorchester by horse-drawn carriage from Salisbury, 40 miles away, in company with his colleague the Honourable Sir John B Bosanquet, and escorted by a, 'numerous cavalcade of javelin-men' who provided their armed escort. Now aged 57, Sir John Williams, who came from a wealthy Cheshire family, was educated at Manchester Grammar School and Trinity College, Cambridge. In 1823 he became MP for the City of Lincoln. On the accession of King William IV in 1830 he was appointed Solicitor-General and Attorney-General to the King's Consort Queen Adelaide. Early in the present year, 1834, he had been advanced to the Bench (i.e. been made a judge), as a Baron of the Exchequer.[1] Now, here he was, mindful of his recent promotion, and anxious to do everything assiduously, and by the book.

Having stopped, briefly, at County Hall in order for their 'Commission' (Order to perform certain duties pertaining to the Dorset Lent Assizes) to be opened and read, the justices proceeded to St Peter's Church for the purpose of attending Divine Service. Here, they heard an 'excellent' sermon, preached by the Reverend John Morton Colson (who was also a magistrate and signatory to the 'Caution'), using a text from the *Holy Bible's* New Testament Book of Romans, Chapter vi, Verse 21: 'What fruit had ye in those things whereof ye are now ashamed? For the end of those things is death.' For those awaiting trial, the implications were obvious. Justice – or at any rate, what passed for justice - was about to be dispensed. The two judges then went their separate ways: the Honourable Sir John Bosanquet to take the lower court of *Nisi Prius*, and Mr Baron Williams to preside over proceedings in the Crown Court.[2] They then retired to their lodgings - a long, narrow building adjoining County Hall on its east side.

Normally, the Dorset Lent Assizes would have attracted but little attention beyond Dorchester and its immediate confines, and having been reported in the local newspapers, and discussed in ale houses and households throughout the town and its immediate vicinity, the events which took place there would quickly have been forgotten. After all, for the gossips, there was always another assize to look forward to! This trial, however, was to be different. It would make the village of Tolpuddle a place of pilgrimage, not to say reverence, and the name 'Loveless' known and revered throughout the world, as being synonymous with the struggle of downtrodden working men and women everywhere.

On Saturday March 15 the Grand Jury was duly sworn in. If it returned a True Bill – in other words, decided that the Indictment of the six Tolpuddle men was valid, then the case would go to trial. As its members included James Frampton, his brother Henry, his step-brother Charles Wollaston, and the Honourable William Ponsonby, who happened to be foreman of the jury and brother-in-law of Lord Melbourne, the outcome was nothing more than a foregone conclusion. In the words of George Loveless himself:

I thought to myself, there is no danger but we shall be found guilty, as we have a special jury for the purpose, selected from among those who are most unfriendly towards us - the grand jury, landowners; the petty jury, land renters. Under such a charge, from such a quarter, self interest alone would induce them to say, 'Guilty.'[3]

Mr Baron Williams began his address by declaring that he had observed from the calendar a great increase in crime. Having devoted some time to the subject of another case on the current list (one of child murder), he then elaborated as follows on the subject of trade unions and the swearing of illegal oaths. It was no light matter, he declared:

...to receive an oath in the secret manner alluded to, especially if it should appear to be for illegal purposes [which it patently was not!], as it is disparaging and bringing into discredit the administration of oaths altogether, thereby affecting that which is essential to the purity of judicial oaths, upon the obligation of which the administration of justice depends.

Openness and publicity of conduct have hitherto been considered the criteria of honesty, and I fear it would be an evil day for this country if the disposition for such openness should fail. All secret societies, which are self-constituted — self-elected, are calculated to shake the foundations of society, and bring the country into extremely perilous circumstances. The misery of these particular cases is this, that men subject themselves to the irresponsible conduct of others, who have no regard for individuals over whom they exercise this authority, and who are the most dangerous persons in the world, to be intrusted with authority: the unhappy men who have been thus misled are in a state of the most wretched subjection and debasement. Gentlemen, of all the persons affected by it, not even excepting the public, the unfortunate persons themselves who are brought into the trammels of these bonds, and have had an oath of this kind administered to them, are affected the worst. Sure I am that in my own experience I have known that they have been compelled by forced oaths to make out of their scanty means contributions to as large an amount as would not be endured if demanded by Government for the service of their country. The arbitrary demands made on them have in many instances exceeded anything before known in this or any other country. Nor does the evil rest here, for when men unite themselves to such societies, the common right of labouring for whom they please is taken from them. This is undoubtedly a very serious subject, and as far as your influence extends I doubt not that every means will be used on your parts for the prevention of this great, and I fear prevalent mischief.

He then begged the Grand Jury to 'find' (make up its mind) as quickly as possible on, 'one or two bills, in order that the court may proceed with the numerous cases which are to be brought before it.'[4] This it did, and the case of the Six Men of Tolpuddle could now go to trial before a 'Petty Jury' consisting (in theory, at least) of twelve good men and true.

Mr Baron Williams would have been well satisfied with his work so far. He had accused the leaders of trade unions, and by implication those of the Tolpuddle union, not only of irresponsibility, but of endangering the very safety of the realm itself. Those members of trade unions who had been 'misled', and 'forced' to swear an oath of allegiance, had become 'unhappy' and 'wretched' as a result. The fact that they were not only wretched and unhappy, but also starving, even prior to their having sworn the oath, appears to have escaped him completely!

The Bill of Indictment against George Loveless and his companions included no less than twelve counts, the first of which contains the essence of what the men were charged with:

> The Jurors for our Lord the King [William IV] upon their Oath present that… [the names of the six men were then duly listed, James Hammett's name being spelt with only one 't'] on the twenty-fourth day of February in the fourth year of the reign of our Sovereign Lord William IV [1834] at the parish aforesaid [of Tolpuddle] in the County aforesaid feloniously and unlawfully did administer and cause to be administered unto one Edward Legg a certain Oath and Engagement purporting and then and there intended to bind the said Edward Legg not to inform or give evidence against any associate confederate or other person of and belonging to a certain unlawful combination and confederacy before that time formed and entered into by and between the said George Loveless, James Loveless, James Brine, James Hammet, Thomas Stanfield, and John Stanfield, and divers other evil disposed persons, and which said Oath and Engagement was then and there taken by the said Edward Legg, against the peace of our said Lord the King, his Crown, and Dignity, and against the form of the Statute in that case made and provided.

This would probably have sufficed, but the prosecuting authorities had seen fit to add another eleven counts, in each of which, the greater part of the text of its predecessor was repeated at length. The result was that all the counts after the first were virtually identical; the Second Count simply declaring that the six men were 'feloniously present', and that they had, 'feloniously aided and assisted at Legg's taking of the oath [Edward Legg, member of the Tolpuddle union, who was shortly to give evidence against the six men]; the Third, that the person who administered the oath was, 'to the Jurors unknown' – i.e. his identity was a mystery; the Ninth referred to Legg being bound by the oath not to divulge the fact that he himself nor, 'any other person or persons' had taken the oath; the Tenth declared that the oath was intended to bind Legg to obeying the, 'orders and commands of a certain body of men not lawfully constituted.' So why was the Indictment so verbose and repetitive? Doubtless, with the idea that, by constantly repeating such words as 'illegal', 'unlawful', 'not lawful', 'evil disposed persons', and 'feloniously', fear would be struck into the heart of the six men, whilst the jurors would be left in no doubt as to what was required of them.

The prosecution had now, at last, put its cards on the table. The men were to be charged, not with creating a trade union, but with administering, and causing to be administered to Edward Legg, an illegal oath. Could the squires or farmers of the county have cared less about whether someone had sworn an illegal oath? Probably not, unless, of course, the result of it was to affect them personally. On the other hand, the creation of a trade union in the heart of rural Dorset – that was a different matter altogether! Now they had the best of both worlds, in that the Six Men of Tolpuddle had unwittingly provided them with the proverbial sprat (the illegal oath) with which to catch the mackerel (the union).

What, it may be asked, could George Loveless and his companions offer in their defence, given that the whole apparatus of the State was ranged so powerfully against them? And what would sustain them, through the gruelling days which lay ahead?

The Dorset County Chronicle made it abundantly clear just whose side *it* was on. 'The emissaries of discontent and sedition [i.e. the unionists]' had 'worked their way', and were, 'endeavouring to seduce the lower orders from the paths of peaceful and productive industry and social order.' However, it did reserve some censure for the present Whig government, which it saw as being, 'very deficient in those qualities of statesmanship which are calculated to inspire public confidence and make people happy,' and as having simply made a bad situation worse.

The newspaper went on to hint at a conspiracy, in which the unionists were simply pawns being manipulated by higher mortals. It had been:

> ...almost invariably the case that revolutions have been set in motion by men of rank and respectability, who, making use of the lower classes as instruments whereby to attain their own purposes, afterwards attempt, without effecting the promises made, to spurn away the living ladder by which they have ascended....

> We look upon these Unions as an alarming evidence of the extent to which social disorganization has proceeded; we regard them as a link in that revolutionary chain, which is surely girding and paralysing the energies of our country; as a part of a system of lawless association that will spread until it has overwhelmed all law and society...

The unionists, said *The Dorset County Chronicle* were, 'deluded'. If their operations were successful, they would stifle trade, commerce, and manufacturing, thereby, 'choking up those resources from whence flows the remuneration of labour.' As a result, 'the tremendously ruinous effect of their combinations' would, 'fall on themselves with peculiar force.'[5]

1. Citrine, Walter (Editor). *The Book of the Martyrs of Tolpuddle, 1834-1934*, p.237.
2. *The Dorset County Chronicle*, 20 March 1834.
3. Loveless, George. *The Victims of Whiggery*, p.9.
4. *The Dorset County Chronicle*, 20 March 1834.
5. Ibid, 6 March 1834.

12

The Trial Begins

The trial of the six men commenced on 17 March 1834 - a Monday. That day in Dorchester there were clouds and intermittent sunshine, with a gentle, southerly breeze. Later, and prophetically, the day became overcast and the sky darkened.[1]

Mr Baron Williams and his retinue had swept into the courthouse by way of the three enormous and imposing wooden, double doors which led directly out onto High West Street. As for George Loveless and his companions, they had been marched from His Majesty's Prison (which Loveless called 'jail'), and locked in a small, single room – described by Loveless as, 'a miserable dungeon' – in the basement of County Hall.[2] Therefore, all that it was necessary for them to do - the door of the cell having been unlocked - was to ascend the seventeen wooden steps which led directly upwards into the dock.

The six men were not the only ones to be imprisoned prior to their trial, for the prosecution's two principal witnesses - who happened both to be labourers from the nearby village of Affpuddle - shared the same fate. John Lock, aged 24, married with two children was one; Edward Legg (already mentioned), aged 36, married with five children, was the other. The Dorchester Prison Records for 7 March 1834 (their date of imprisonment) contained the entry, 'Wollaston [magistrate], for want of sureties, to give evidence.' (In other words, the reason for the two men being imprisoned was that they were unable to provide a responsible person to guarantee their appearance in court).[3]

One may picture the scene: the judge, aloft in his chair beneath the Royal Arms of King George III (father of the present king, William IV), from which the court derived its authority. Alongside him were benches reserved for court recorders and trainee judges. Below him, in the well of the court, sat the teams for the defence and for the prosecution. In the enclosed gallery to his left were seated the twelve members of the jury: all of whom were men, and all of them yeomen (men possessing free land of an annual value of 40 shillings, who by this fact are qualified to be jurors), except for one, who is described as 'farmer'. There were no working men on the jury – how could there be, given such preconditions? – and this lent a further bias to the proceedings before they had even begun! In other words, the jury was there to give the answers which the prosecution demanded of it.

The gallery above the judge, and to his right, was reserved for friends of the judge, and also for those members of the Grand Jury who wished to attend; though this was not compulsory. (It is likely that Magistrate James Frampton was among their number, eagerly waiting to see the goal which he had set himself achieved, and the Tolpuddle men convicted). At the end of this gallery was the judge's robing room. It is also probable that this is where newspaper reporters sat.

The raised platform at the far end of the Court, opposite the judge's seat, was set aside for any member of the public who wished to attend, of whom there were many. In fact, the Assizes were of such interest in days when entertainment was limited, that the queue of excited and inquisitive would-be spectators stretched right along the street. Those fortunate enough to obtain admission to the limited space that was available, made the most of their opportunity, participating noisily in the proceedings, and eating and drinking food which they had brought with them. Clearly, they were here for the duration! In front of them sat members of the accuseds' families.

At a signal from the judge, a bell was rung to instruct the guard to bring up the prisoners - the Six Men of Tolpuddle - who were herded together into the raised dock, along with their guard, there to await their fate.

Counsel for the Prosecution was Mr Edward J Gambier. For the defence, Mr S Derbyshire (who had been called to the Bar four years previously) represented George Loveless, his brother James, and Thomas Standfield. Mr George Medd Butt represented John Standfield, James Hammett, and James Brine. Because no official record of the trial exists, *The Dorset County Chronicle* and other contemporary media coverage provide the next best sources of information.

Opening the case for the prosecution, Mr Gambier drew the attention of the Jury to the Act, 39 Geo.III c.79, of 1799, which declared as illegal any society which administered an oath which was not required by law.[4] Gambier also referred to another Act, 57 Geo III c.19, sec.25, which dealt with seditious meetings and assemblies, and which he declared, 'was to the same purport.' What Gambier failed to mention was that the Indictment of the Six men of Tolpuddle was in fact framed on the 1797 Mutiny Act (37 Geo III c.70), which was highly inappropriate in the circumstances, it having been drawn up as previously mentioned, with the specific intention of pre-empting mutiny and sedition in the armed services.

The first witness to be examined was John Lock, a member of the Tolpuddle union.[5] Lock was employed as gardener in the employ of James Frampton, and on this account, hardly to be relied upon to give testimony that was impartial. A day or two prior to Christmas 1833, Lock had visited Tolpuddle, where he met James Brine (one of the six men, not the parish constable of the same name), whom he knew. Brine had led him to a house opposite to the one where Thomas Stanfield lived, and invited him in. (This was the house of John Daniel, agricultural labourer, who was also a member of the Tolpuddle union).[6] Lock, however, declined the offer, and went on his way. One evening, two to three weeks later, when Lock was at work at Affpuddle, he encountered Brine once again, in company with James Hammett. Lock was about to finish work for the day, when Brine invited him to accompany himself and Hammett to Tolpuddle. This time Lock accepted the invitation. On the journey they met with four other men: Edward Legg, Richard Percy (sometimes spelt Pearcy), Henry Courtney, and Elias Riggs (all members of the Tolpuddle union),[7] and Lock heard one of these men ask whether, 'there would not be something to pay.' The answer was yes, 'there would be a shilling to pay on entering [i.e. the Union], and a penny a week afterwards.'

On arriving at Tolpuddle they entered a room, whereupon John Stanfield joined them. George Loveless and his brother James were also present. One of them (Lock was not sure who), asked if he, Lock, and the four other men who had met with them on the road, were ready to have blindfolds placed over their eyes. They agreed, and were then led through a passage into another room where 'a paper' was read to them, the words of which Lock did not recollect. They were then asked to kneel down when another paper was read; again, by whom he did not know, but the voice on each occasion appeared to have been the same. Lock thought the second reading was from the *Holy Bible*. When the blindfolds were removed, Lock noticed that in the corner of the room was a picture of a skeleton. Looking at this picture, James Loveless had said, 'Remember your end.'

The men were then blindfolded, and required to kneel. They were read to again and, 'afterwards desired to kiss a book', when their eyes were then 'unblinded'. Lock then saw all the six prisoners currently present in the dock. He noticed that James Loveless, 'had then a different dress [attire] from what he now has on.' The rules were then read out to them, 'I think by George Loveless.' Lock said that he did not know the exact meaning of the rules, except (as he already knew) that a fee of one shilling was payable on entering the society, and a penny a week afterwards. This, 'to support the men who were out of work — those who had struck [i.e. gone on strike] - till their masters should raise their wages.' Lock was told that if the men intended to strike they, 'need not name it to our masters, because they [the masters] would have a letter sent to them [i.e. by the Union] acquainting them of it.' Lock told the court that he duly paid his shilling to George Loveless.

Cross-examined by Mr Butt for the Defence, Lock stated that he had known John Stanfield for three or four years. He also knew Hammett and Brine, and to his knowledge the three men, 'always bore a good character.' Cross-examined by the Judge, Lock declared that the apparel which Loveless had been attired in was, 'more like a surplice than a smock frock.'

It was now the turn of Edward Legg (also a member of the Tolpuddle Union) to be examined by the prosecution. Having confirmed that he was a labourer, also from Affpuddle, Legg stated that one evening, shortly before the previous Christmas, he had been at home when Brine and Hammett had knocked on his window pane and asked him to accompany them to Tolpuddle. Was this in order that he should swear an oath, Legg enquired, for he was already aware that there had been, 'some swearing in of our people at Tolpuddle'? Whereupon, James Brine told him that, 'they wished to see how many men they could assemble together.' What were the names of 'the persons they were going to swear?' asked Legg. Brine then gave the names of three individuals: Percy, Courtney, and another.

Having arrived at Tolpuddle, said Legg, they were conducted by Brine and Hammett to Thomas Standfield's house. Here, they all went upstairs into a room, where Thomas Standfield, John Standfield, and George and James Loveless were present. From here on, Legg's testimony is much the same as Lock's: he remembered being blindfolded; kissing the book (*Holy Bible*), and something being said about, 'our souls being plunged into eternity if we did not keep the secret - if we disclosed any thing that we heard and that was done there.' Legg also recalled that in the room was a picture, 'which represented Death.' Also, the words 'Society' and 'Brothers' being used after they had been sworn. Cross-examined by Mr Butt for the Defence, Legg declared that he knew all the prisoners; that, 'they are all hard-working men, and I never heard a word against any of them.'

In *The Victims of Whiggery*, George Loveless declared that although Edward Legg had sworn that James Hammett was present at this meeting, this was not in fact the case.[8] Years later, James Hammett himself would confirm this, by disclosing that it was actually his younger brother John who was present on that fateful occasion. James, however, chose to remain silent, in order to protect John, then aged only 19, and his wife Elizabeth (née Brown) who was heavily pregnant at the time.

The next witness was Mrs Frances Whetham, the wife of a painter Mr James Whetham of Dorchester. Cross-examined by the Prosecution, she told how, some time in the previous year, James Loveless had visited her husband's shop and had asked for something to be painted, for which he had the design - written on two pieces of paper - which he left with her. 'One of the papers represented Death,' she said, 'and the other a Skeleton.' Loveless told her that the background of the paintings must be dark, and their height was to be 6 feet. Over the head of the figure of Death, Loveless said, were to be painted the words 'Remember thine end.' He said the paintings were intended for a society, but more than this he did not say.

James Whetham was now examined. He stated that when James Loveless asked him whether he had completed the paintings, he had replied, no, and that he, 'could not make out the meaning of the designs.' For what purpose were the paintings required? For a society, said Loveless, a society of their own; which was a secret of theirs. On hearing this, Whetham told him that he, 'could not undertake to execute the paintings.'

John Cox, turnkey (under-jailor), described how, when George Loveless had arrived at His Majesty's Prison, Dorchester, on 25 February 1834, he (Cox) had discovered, in his (Loveless's) pocket, two printed papers, a letter, and a key. Robert Andrews, governor of the jail, confirmed that the papers and the key (currently exhibited before the court) had been handed over to him by Cox. Officer John Toomer described how Magistrate James Frampton had, in turn, handed the key over to him, whereupon he had called at the house of George Loveless, where he was admitted by Loveless's wife Elizabeth. 'I applied the key to a box… which it unlocked; the box contained two books; Brine [the parish constable] was with me when I took the books out of the box...' Toomer duly delivered the books (now exhibited before the court) to James Frampton, who duly passed them on to Mr Coombs (perhaps a court official).

Constable James Brine, who described himself as 'a tithingman' (collector of tithes), affirmed that yes, he had accompanied Toomer to the house of George Loveless. As to the books: one contained the names of those who had taken the (illegal) oath and joined the Tolpuddle union (James Frampton to Viscount Howick, 3 May 1834); the other contained the rules and regulations of the Union.[9]

The letter found in the pocket of George Loveless, when he had been committed to prison, was now read out in court. Headed 'Bere Heath', and dated 1 February 1834, it was addressed to George Loveless and signed 'Geo. Romaine, Secretary'. Clearly, Romaine was evidently in the process of setting up another trade union at Bere Regis:

> Brother - We met this evening for the purpose of forming our committee; them were 16 present, of whom 10 were chosen, namely, President, Vice-President, Secretary, Treasurer, Warden, Conductor, 3 outside Guardians, and 1 inside Guardian. All seemed united in heart, and expressed their approval of the meeting. Father and Hallett [presumably a misspelling of 'Hammett'] wished very much to join us, but wish it not to be known. I advised them to come Tuesday evening at six o'clock and I would send for you to come at that time if possible and enter them that they may be gone before the company come. I received your note this morning, which gave me great encouragement, and am led to acknowledge the force [strength] of the union.

The 'Caution' which had been displayed in Tolpuddle by the magistrates, warning against the inducing of labourers to join illegal societies or unions, 'to which they bind themselves by unlawful oaths,' was also read to the jury, as were the 'General Laws' of the Tolpuddle union, together with the relevant legal statutes.[10]

❖ ❖ ❖

Meanwhile, beyond the confines of the Court, life went on as usual. A ladies' boarding school, situated on the Esplanade, Weymouth and, 'conducted by

Mrs Twigg and daughters,' advertised their terms in *The Dorset County Chronicle*. 'Full board... with the French language and a general course of English education, including writing and arithmetic, geography and the use of the globes' was offered for the annual sum of 30 guineas.

In Dorchester, 'in a healthy part of the town,' an apartment was advertised suitable for, 'a single lady or gentleman (or two sisters), with sitting-room, bed-room, attic and kitchen.' Mr Pouncy advertised, 'a constant situation and good wages' for a journeyman saddler and harness-maker, provided that he was, 'a respectable man, of steady habits, who is a perfect master of the business.' At Wareham, a man and his wife (or alternatively, a 'steady woman') were wanted, 'without encumbrance', to manage a dairy, not exceeding twenty cows.

Times of meeting for Mr Farquaharson's, Mr Tobin's, and Mr Portman's hounds were displayed, and for Mr Bastard's harriers (dogs used for hunting hares), which would meet on Thursday 6 March at Blandford Racecourse.

At the other end of the social scale, under the heading 'Dorchester Poor', the accounts of the Dorchester Hospital were published. Details included payments for beef, veal, pork, cheese, oatmeal, flour, potatoes and vegetables, as well as for table beer, soap, tobacco and snuff. It was reported that there were currently thirty-eight paupers in the hospital (four being over the age of 70 years, and seven below the age of 20), of whom seventeen were male and twenty-one female. 'Maintenance of each pauper per week, 8s.7½d.'[11]

1. National Meteorological Archive, Great Moor House, Bittern Road, Sowton, Exeter, UK.
2. Loveless, George. *The Victims of Whiggery*, p.8.
3. Dorchester Prison Records, Dorset History Centre, Microfilm R878.
5. British Library: *Frampton Papers*, Ms.41567L Folio 141.
4. Citrine, Walter (Editor). *The Book of the Martyrs of Tolpuddle, 1834-1934*, p.22.
6. British Library, op.cit., Frampton to Melbourne, 5 March 1834, Ms. 41567L Folio 141.
7. Ibid, Ms 41567L, Folio 141.
8. Loveless, op.cit., p.7.
9. British Library, op.cit., Frampton to Melbourne, 5 March 1834, Ms.41567L Folio 141.
10. *The Dorset County Chronicle*, 20 March 1834.
11. This latter sum, incidentally, was more than the current weekly wage of an agricultural labourer! See *The Dorset County Chronicle*, 3 April 1834.

13

The Case for the Defence: Summing Up: Verdict

Mr Butt, acting in defence of John Standfield, James Hammett, and James Brine, argued that the evidence produced by the prosecution was not sufficient to warrant His Lordship's putting the case before the jury. He reiterated the preamble to Act 37 Geo.III, c.123 ('Mutiny Act') upon which the indictment was framed, but pointed out that this Act had been 'very properly framed' in order to discourage mutiny and sedition amongst soldiers and seamen at a time when the country was in great danger. In other words, it was inappropriate to invoke this Act against his clients.

In defence of George and James Loveless and Thomas Standfield, Mr Derbishire also submitted that there was insufficient evidence to send the case to the jury. In regard to the swearing of the oath, the only evidence was that of, 'two stupid witnesses,' who told the court that:

> …at a certain meeting where they had chosen voluntarily to blind themselves, some words were uttered by someone chosen [whom] they did not know, about something they did not understand, but in which they recollected the words 'eternity' and 'soul,' for what purpose [these words were] introduced they could not imagine.

It was Mr Derbishire's opinion that, 'this was not such evidence of an oath that would sustain the indictment.' As for the Tolpuddle union, what evidence was there to show that the prisoners had formed an unlawful association within the meaning of the Act 37 Geo.III, c.123: an Act which was principally concerned with the suppression of mutiny and sedition, and with the disturbing of the public peace? Did not the rules and regulations of a society, which had been found in the pocket of one of the prisoners (i.e. George Loveless), prove that the society to which those rules applied, 'was the reverse of an illegal combination or confederacy, within the meaning of the Act or in violation of any known law?' In fact, as he saw it, the objective of the 'Agricultural Friendly Society' [a misquotation – the correct name being 'The Friendly Society of Labourers'] of Tolpuddle:

> …was to provide a fund, or kind of Agricultural Savings Bank for mutual succour and maintenance in the hour of need. The prisoners were poor, labouring men, having wives and families with helpless children to support. They were liable to be thrown out of work, to sickness and various accidents, and he could not understand how an association to provide against seasons of scarcity and obviate starvation could be deemed an unlawful combination.
>
> The poor man had as much right to protect the property he had in his labour, as the rich had to protect his accumulations of wealth, and it would be rather a hard measure of justice, and never could have been intended by the Legislature, to treat men as felons and condemn them to transportation, whose only crime was conspiring to protect each other from the evils of probable starvation. His Lordship was aware, that the wisdom and benevolence of the Legislature had caused the whole of the laws against combinations to be repealed. There had long ceased to be any restriction upon masters combining to reduce the rate of wages, or upon workmen to raise them. The prisoners were entitled to this fact in their favour.

Mr Derbishire, in his appeal to the Court, had spoken with eloquence and feeling. The question was, would he and his colleague Mr Butt be successful in their efforts on behalf of the prisoners?

According to George Loveless, the judge then inquired if the prisoners had anything to say. Whereupon the former forwarded to him, 'the following short defence, in writing':

> My Lord, if we have violated any law, it was not done intentionally: we have injured no man's reputation, character, person or property: we were uniting together to preserve ourselves, our wives, and our children, from utter degradation and starvation. We challenge any man, or number of men to prove that we have acted, or intend to act different from the above statement.

The judge asked Loveless if he wished this note to be read aloud to the court. Said he:

I answered, 'Yes.' It was then mumbled over to a part of the jury, in such an inaudible manner, that although I knew what was there, I could not comprehend it.[1]

✤ ✤ ✤

In his summing up the judge, Mr Baron Williams, emphasised to the jury that they must satisfy themselves that the oath which Legg had taken, and which had been administered to other members of the society, was an illegal one. If the purpose of that Act was to bind Legg, 'not to divulge the secrets of the society,' then it was his Lordship's view that the taking of it would come within the meaning of the Act.

The jury was also asked to consider whether James Loveless's outer garment, worn at the swearing in, 'which resembled a clergyman's surplice, was not intended to give a degree of solemnity and additional force to the proceedings,' and whether the representations of a skeleton and of a Death's head were also, 'intended to strike awe on the minds of the persons to whom the oath was administered.' The judge observed that in the ceremony where the oath was taken, 'mention was made of the soul and eternity.' If, therefore, the jury was satisfied that the oath was intended, 'as an obligation on the conscience of the person taking it,' then once again, in his view, it came within the meaning of the Act.

After speculating on the significance of the skeleton and Death's head, his Lordship pointed out to the jury that the rules of the Tolpuddle union ('Society') spoke of the, 'violation of an obligation,' which appeared to be a reference to the oath, the breaking of which the union would consider a crime. He then:

> …read from a book belonging to the Society the names of several persons (the prisoners among others) who had contributed to its funds; leaving the Jury to draw their conclusions from these facts and the whole chain of evidence which had been repeated to them.

As they stood in the dock for hour after hour, listening to the court proceedings, the six accused men could not have failed to notice a small door in one of its side panels. If a prisoner was declared to be innocent, it is believed that this door would be unlocked, to allow him or her to walk free. The question now was, would the door be opened, or would it remain locked? The answer was not long in coming, for having deliberated over the evidence for, 'about five minutes,' the jury found all the prisoners guilty. They would now await their sentence.[2]

Two days later, on the morning of 17 March 1834, Mr Baron Williams addressed the prisoners. The case put forward by the six men's defence counsel, he said, did, 'not amount in point of law to objection to the conviction or the evidence.' In other words, he dismissed the defence's case. He then went on to make insinuations about the motives of the convicted men, implying that they had a sinister intent, and were a danger to the State. 'The secret intentions of men can only be judged by others from their conduct,' he said. But whatever they may have been, 'the necessary effects of their acts upon the public security is of such a nature that the public security requires that some public example should be made... [i.e. of the men],' as an, 'example and warning' to others.

Mr Baron Williams believed that, 'the conduct of men who secretly withdraw themselves from all public notice, is likely only to grow worse in consequence of such withdrawal.' The evidence upon which they had been convicted was, to his mind, 'perfectly satisfactory. Now, for the sake of, 'the security of the country, and the maintenance of the laws, on the upholding of which the welfare of the country depends,' it was necessary for him to pass on them, 'the sentence required by those laws.' Having, 'deliberated well and seriously' upon the evidence produced, and upon the nature of the crime, he felt he had no discretion in the matter. Accordingly, he informed the men:

> I am bound to pronounce on you the sentence which the Act of Parliament has imposed. I therefore adjudge that you, and each of you, be transported to such places beyond the seas as His Majesty's Council in their discretion shall see fit for the term of seven years.

In regard to the judge's behaviour towards the Six Men of Tolpuddle, in modern parlance, the phrases 'Conspiracy Theory', and 'Smear Campaign' are those which come most readily to mind.

---

1. George Loveless. *The Victims of Whiggery*, p.9.
2. *The Dorset County Chronicle*, 20 March 1834.

14

Others Sentenced at the Same Assize

It is interesting to compare the sentences handed down to the Six Men of Tolpuddle with those handed down to other prisoners at the Dorset 1834 Lent Assizes: there being fifty in total, of whom twelve were women, and nine under the age of 20 years.

Thomas Horlock was awarded two months imprisonment for stealing four fowls at Pimperne; as was Caroline Steward (with hard labour) for stealing at Milborne [St Andrew], two rummer [large drinking] glasses and a cheese knife; Elias Gosney, charged with entering a wood at Cranborne, armed, for the purpose of destroying game, was found guilty and sentenced to prison and hard labour for three calendar months; Jane Stacey was charged with the wilful murder of a male bastard child on the 21st of July. She pleaded guilty, and was sentenced to six calendar months imprisonment. For the above persons, therefore, their crime was considered to be a lesser one than that for which the Tolpuddle men had been convicted.

The following received the same sentence as the Tolpuddle six, that of seven years transportation, 'beyond the seas'. This, in practice, meant Australia, - transportation to the American colonies having ceased following the War of American Independence, 1775-83. Augustus Moores, John Hardy, and Samuel Best were charged with stealing a trunk containing various articles of jewellery and wearing apparel from a cart at Wareham; Augustus Moores, together with Samuel Best and Joseph Bishop, with stealing at Wareham a quantity of earthenware; Augustus Moores also with stealing a blue and white cotton shirt at Wareham; Eliza Squires, for stealing from the shop of Thomas Bascombe of Dorchester a table-cloth and about 30 yards of silk; Dan Norman (brother of Benjamin), for, 'breaking and entering a warehouse of Mr James Edwards at Bridport, and stealing a bag, some cheese, lard and soap.'

The following prisoners received a sentence in excess of that given to the Tolpuddle six. Isaac Row, for breaking into the house of Edward Seymour, of Bridport, and stealing a silver cup and various gold and silver coins, received one calendar month's imprisonment with hard labour, followed by transportation for fourteen years. Robert Daubeney, for stealing a mare at North Poorton, and for stealing a mare at Loders; Thomas Strange and James Vincent, for, 'having feloniously stolen' three lambs, the property of Philip Peater of Piddletrenthide, received transportation for life. Robert Trent, Joseph Luther, William Short, Robert Manual, James White, and John Stickland, for assembling, armed with sticks, 'to assist in running [smuggling] of prohibited goods at Tyneham,' were all sentenced to death.

Amongst those acquitted by the court were: Sophie Goddard, charged with, 'feloniously, unlawfully, and maliciously, attempting to suffocate her newly-born female bastard child at the parish of Bloxworth.' The case was not proven. Nonetheless, the judge reminded her that she had lost a woman's most valuable possession – her virtue. Also acquitted were Mary Galpine Smith, charged with concealing the birth of a bastard child; John Trowbridge, charged with attempting to commit bestiality.[1]

The proceedings of the court were, therefore, by no means a pre-emptory affair, and pains were taken to ascertain the true facts of the case. However, the majority of the crimes committed would have been considered trivial by today's standards, and the sentences passed, to be, in the main, disproportionately excessive.

It should be emphasised that not everybody travelling to Australia in the year 1834 was doing so in order to be punished, the British Government being anxious to encourage the colonisation of that continent, rather than leave a vacuum which other colonial powers might fill. This is reflected by the following advertisement, from the month of March's pages of *The Dorset County Chronicle*:

EMIGRATION,
FOR HOBART TOWN, VAN DIEMEN'S LAND,
and SYDNEY, NEW SOUTH WALES,
To SAIL early in the Spring,

THE Beautiful fast-Sailing and well Armed New Packet SHIP, *ORWELL*, 400 Tons Burthen; this fine Ship is lying in the St. Catherine's [Katharine's] Docks, has been expressly fitted up with spacious and elegant Cabin for parties proceeding as passengers to these flourishing Colonies. The steerage Berths are very superior, having seven feet heighth [old spelling] between deck, and she carries a Surgeon. The climate of New South Wales and Van Diemen's Land, is considered one of the finest in the World, and as Wages very high and Provisions remarkably cheap, persons of common industry may now realize Ease and Independence.

The following important information has been published lately by His Majesty's Commissioners for Emigration; Pensioners of the army may receive four years Pension by way of commutation, to enable them to emigrate to New South Wales and Van Diemen's Land; unmarried females between the age of 15 and 30, may obtain a free gift of 8 pounds, towards the expense of their passage; Mechanics and artisans may (if married) obtain a loan of £20 for the same purpose.[2]

For further particulars apply on board, or to CHARLES DODD and Co., 46, Lime Street, London.

Two months later, again through the pages of *The Dorset County Chronicle*, John Masson, also of Lime Street, London, announced the departure of the following ships:

For *Hobart Town* and *Launceston*, Van Diemen's Land, the fine ship *JANET*, 300 Tons, S.C. Matheson Commander;

For *Hobart Town*, Van Diemen's, Land and *Sydney*, New South Wales, the ship *WILLIAM*, 350 tons, H. Sowerby Commander;

For *Sydney*, New South Wales direct, the ship *GOVERNOR HARCOURT*, William Doulty Commander;

All loading in St Katherine['s] Dock, London. Married Agricultural Labourers of good character, emigrating with their Wives and Children. Will be allowed a loan from Government to aid them in paying their passage.

For the Six Men of Tolpuddle, no such luxuries were afforded, the terrible privations suffered by them in Australasia being recounted, in graphic detail, by George Loveless in his account entitled *The Victims of Whiggery*, and by four of his five companions in *The Horrors of Transportation: A Narrative of the*

Sufferings of Jas. Loveless, Jas. Brine, and Thomas and John Standfield. This will be discussed shortly.

1. *The Dorset County Chronicle*, 6 March and 20 March 1834.
2. Ibid, 6 March 1834.
3. Ibid, 1 May, 1834.

15

Melbourne and Frampton Turn the Screw

Home Secretary Lord Melbourne, and Magistrate James Frampton were determined that even though the trial was over, they were not prepared to let the matter rest; neither were they to be permitted to let it rest, for there were many in the country, from all walks of life, who burned with indignation at the injustices which the Six Men of Tolpuddle had suffered. On 27 March 1834, only eight days after the conclusion of the trial, Melbourne asked Frampton for further, and better particulars of the six convicted Tolpuddle men, anticipating that when Parliament reassembled after the Easter recess, he might well have to face questions in the House of Commons about the recent events which had taken place at the Dorchester Court of Assize.

Accordingly, on 29 March 1834, Frampton replied to Melbourne, saying that this was not the first brush that George Loveless had had with the law. Whilst acknowledging the fact that George and James Loveless, and Thomas and John Standfield were Methodists (the first two being preachers, and the third an occasional preacher), both the Loveless brothers, said Frampton, had been, 'very active in the riots in the winter of 1830.'

Thomas Standfield, said Frampton, was, 'a very discontented man' who, 'if any disturbance [was] going on, he is sure to be in it'; John Standfield he described as being, 'very saucy' and also, 'ready for any disturbance'; James Hammett, at the age of 18, had been, 'convicted of felony in stealing iron at the Easter Sessions [Assizes], 1829, and sentenced to Four Months Imprisonment with Hard Labour.' He was, 'always a very idle man and ready for mischief'; James Brine had, 'behaved well and tried to keep out of the riots of 1830... but since that time has become very idle and kept company with James Hammett. He was offered work last winter, but did not undertake it.' Since then, Brine had been, 'wandering about... under the pretext of seeking work.' However, there was, 'every reason to believe he has been employed during all that time by the Lovelesses and Stanfields [incorrectly spelt], with James Hammett, in enticing people to join the Union.'

Frampton also referred to the Union's membership list which he had previously sent to Lord Melbourne. This showed that no less than seven persons of the name Loveless were members, all of whom, he was informed, were related. Frampton had also learned (as previously stated) that John Loveless, a flax dresser of Burton Bradstock near Bridport in East Dorset, had supplied his younger brother George, 'with the Rules and with every information relating to the Society ['Friendly Society of Labourers'],' which he himself (John) had received from his own union, the Flax Dressers' Trade Union at Leeds (Yorkshire). 'No doubt is entertained in this neighbourhood,' said Frampton, 'that the six men in question were the ring leaders of the whole [affair].' He also pointed out that George Romaine, Secretary of the Tolpuddle union, was a Methodist preacher and owner of a meeting house on nearby Bere Heath. (The link between Methodism and trade unionism will be discussed shortly).[1]

When Melbourne then demanded evidence of corroboration for the Lovelesses' involvement in the riots of 1830, all that Frampton could produce was hearsay. That very morning (2 April 1834) he had spoken with, 'a very respectable farmer of the Parish of Tolpuddle,' who told him that at the time of the riots of November 1830, all the labourers of the Parish of Tolpuddle had assembled one morning before daybreak. He (the farmer) approached them and asked them whether any of his own labourers were present. At this, George Loveless, 'to whose voice he can swear,' replied, 'Some of them are here and we have sent for the rest.' Continued Frampton:

My informant, together with the other farmers who were by that time present, told the labourers that, although they would not promise them any particular sum, if they went to their work quietly, they should have the same pay as was agreed to be given in other parishes. On which George Loveless said that the first man who started [i.e., indicated that he agreed with the farmers] should have his head cracked.

It was at this time light enough for the farmers to see who was there. James Loveless [George's younger brother] was also very active, appeared much dissatisfied and tried to persuade the men to go to join the mob which had assembled at Piddletown [Puddletown], a village about two miles off. At last, however, by persuasion and threatening [by the authorities] to take down the names of every man who left the parish [of Tolpuddle for Puddletown], the labourers did not go to Piddletown but returned to their work.[2]

It has to be said, that this is the unsubstantiated evidence of only one person - the farmer - and that his portrayal of George Loveless as a potentially violent man is entirely out of character with the known facts about him.

Melbourne now wrote to Frampton on the subject of James Hammett's conviction in 1829. Frampton responded by enclosing a copy of the relevant certificate from the Dorchester Prison Records.[3]   In the event, Melbourne chose to ignore the 'evidence' produced by Frampton against both George Loveless and James Hammett, which he regarded as flimsy.

❖ ❖ ❖

Nevertheless, Frampton was unable to contain his delight at the conviction of the six men, and he now proceeded to make the lives of their families, who were already suffering through the absence of their breadwinners, a perfect misery (and also, no doubt, those families of all the fifty men who were members of the Tolpuddle union). In his letter to Melbourne of 29 March 1834, he declared that:

> The conviction and prompt execution of the sentence of trans-portation has given the greatest satisfaction to all the Higher classes, and will, I have no doubt, have a very great effect amongst the Labourers; as great pains have been taken to instil into their minds that the men would undergo only a slight punishment; as the Unions were so powerful the Government would not venture to put the Sentence in force.[4]

On 12 April 1834, George Loveless's wife Elizabeth wrote to a Mr Richard Holland Goode of Coventry, a local businessman and philanthropist[5], describing the straightened circumstances in which she and the families of the other five men now found themselves. 'We are now left destitute of any thing for our support,' she said. They had applied to Magistrate James Frampton for relief; yet their application had been denied, and they were advised to apply, instead, to the 'union club'. When they applied to Mr C B Wollaston (Chairman of the Quarter Sessions) at County Hall, Dorchester, the response was the same, 'for they meant us to suffer for the offences of our husbands.' Tolpuddle's Overseer of the Poor was equally unyielding, telling them that they and their children, 'must suffer because our husbands had committed such a heinous crime.'

Finally, when Elizabeth told the authorities at the Dorchester workhouse that she, 'could not remain to see the children perish for want,' and that she would rather go to service [presumably at the workhouse] and leave the children in the care of the authorities, she was told that if she embarked upon this course of action, she too would be punished by transportation. 'Had it not been for kind friends,' said Elizabeth, the children would indeed have perished for want.

Elizabeth proceeded to acquaint Mr Goode with the facts relating to the families. She herself had three children; her brother-in-law James Loveless and his wife Sarah had two; Thomas and Dinah [which Elizabeth spelt Dianna] Standfield had five;; James and Harriett Hammett had one, aged 14 months; Catherine, the widowed mother of James Brine, had four, for whom James had been the sole source of support. (John Standfield, like James Brine, was as yet unmarried). Elizabeth declared that had it not been for a gentleman from London who visited, enquired as to their circumstances, and gave them £2. 3s. each, then she could not tell what she would have done. Elizabeth was also concerned for the welfare of other members of the Tolpuddle union who had been victimised: William Way, with seven children; William Lake, with six children; William Hamet (Hammett), who was, 'out of employ because he would not agree with the farmer for 4 shillings per week for a twelve month.'

Here, it is necessary to mention the generosity shown to the Loveless family by Sally Legg, wife of Edward, who had testified against the Martyrs at their trial. In the words of a subsequent report in Dorset's *Daily Echo* newspaper, this lady:

> …rendered many little acts of kindness to the stricken families of the labourers, and she was always looked upon with the greatest of affection by them. To the children of one of the Loveless brothers she gave food when they (the family) were hungry, and, in return, the wife gave her a chair from the little furniture she possessed.[6]

The letter to Mr Goode was signed by Elizabeth and Sarah Loveless and Harriett Hammett (spelt 'Haryet Hamet') with their names, and by Dianne Standfield (spelt 'Dianna') and Catherine Brine who made the mark of an 'X'.[7]

On 3 May 1834, Frampton wrote to Viscount Howick. It was perfectly true, he said, that he and his fellow justices had refused to sanction any parochial relief to the wives and families of the six 'convicts' on the (irrelevant and probably spurious) grounds that, according to the gaoler at Dorchester Prison, the men had been supplied by their wives, 'with more food than they could consume' during the time of their imprisonment in the gaol. Frampton had also told the applicants (for relief) that, as the leaders of the union had promised to maintain all the families of those who joined the organisation, the families should therefore, 'apply to those leaders, and require of them to keep their promise.' This would have the added advantage of reducing the burden on the parish.

Frampton informed Howick that it had been privately explained to the Overseer of the Poor that although he was not to offer relief, he was to watch over the parties, and to assist them, 'if he found they really were distressed.' As a result, said Frampton, the overseer had given relief to the family of George Loveless, but his action had, 'immediately caused the others to apply for relief, which he refused.' However, since that time the overseer had occasionally relieved all the families, with the exception of that of Catherine Brine.

Frampton reported that very soon after the first application for relief, a person called Newman (a cabinet maker, to whom Elizabeth Loveless had referred in her letter to Mr Goode) had travelled down from London, and given relief (money) to the families. He, Frampton, had reason to believe that the families were now being maintained by the union. The Reverend Dr Warren, Vicar of Tolpuddle had also received some money, from a Mr Morrison, which he had distributed to the families. For these reasons, said Frampton, the justices had forbidden the overseer from granting parochial relief to any person listed in George Loveless's book as having, 'taken the illegal oath and … joined the union.' He also noted that none of these persons had, 'ever in any way acknowledged their error, or expressed any sorrow at having joined the unions.'

Frampton refuted the suggestion that any, 'person of the vestry' (i.e. minister of the church) had ever threatened the women with transportation if they left their children and went into service. The justices had, however, recommended to the farmers, 'that every encouragement should be given to those labourers who did not join the union by increasing their wages, and placing them in all the most profitable work, so that they may feel the advantage of their good conduct, by making a marked difference between them and the unionists….' On the other hand, on no account were they, at present, 'to make any addition to the wages of the latter, lest it should have the slightest appearance of being done through fear.'[8]

It was at about this time that the London Central Dorchester Committee was

81

created, consisting of sixteen members, all of whom were working men. Its task was to organise protests against the perceived injustice which the six Tolpuddle men had suffered, and also to attend to the welfare of their families. One of their number was Robert Loveless, younger brother of George, and older brother of James. Robert was a flax dresser by trade, who would naturally have been concerned for the plight of his two siblings.[9]

1. British Library: *Frampton Papers*. Frampton to Melbourne, 29 March 1834, Ms41567L Folio 161.
2. Ibid, Frampton to Melbourne, 29 March 1834, Ms.41567L Folio 161.
3. Dorset History Centre, Microfilm No. R878.
4. British Library, op.cit., Frampton to Melbourne, 29 March 1834, Ms. 41567L Folio 161.
5. Coventry City Record Office.
6. The report went on to state that the chair was now in the possession of Mr Andrew Legg of Weymouth, a grandson of Edward Legg. Dorset Daily Echo, 1 September 1934.
7. Elizabeth Loveless to Mr Richard Goode, Butt's Lane, Coventry, 12 April 1834. Quoted in Citrine, Walter (Editor). *The Book of the Martyrs of Tolpuddle, 1834-1934*, p.34.
8. British Library, op.cit., Frampton to Viscount Howick, 3 May 1834, Ms.41567L Folio 171.
9. Citrine, Walter (Editor). *The Book of the Martyrs of Tolpuddle*, p.236.

16

Tolpuddle:
George Loveless's Home Village

The names 'Loveles', 'Lovelas', and 'Lovelace' (all interchangable with Loveless) appear in the Dorset's 16th century Tudor Muster Rolls (lists of adult men available for military service, together with their available weaponry). For example, John Loveles of Alton Pancras is described as an able bodied man having a bow and ½ sheaf of arrows; whereas William Lovelas of Sydling St Nicholas was able to furnish a bow and a full sheaf of arrows. However, there are no 'Loveless' entries (or variations of that name) for Tolpuddle, and when Lovelesses first arrived in Tolpuddle is uncertain.

Tolpuddle, Crown Inn. Photo: Audrey Wirdnam.

Tolpuddle is a parish slightly in excess of 2,000 acres, in which the surrounding landscape is overwhelmingly farmland underlain with chalk. This falls away from the north side, down towards the river valley and its extensive water meadows, where the flow of water, in George Loveless's time, was controlled by sluice gates. It is not surprising, therefore, that the majority of the working men of the village were, like him, agricultural labourers. However, many other trades were represented including that of: carpenter, shoemaker, publican, thatcher, baker, carter, bricklayer (of which there were five), journeyman (hired labourer), dairyman (of which there were three), blacksmith, carrier, grocer, and brick maker.

Ploughing at nearby Stinsford. Photo (by W Pouncy): Dorset County Museum.

The majority of the inhabitants of Tolpuddle village lived on either side of the street (the main road running from the direction of Dorchester, 5 miles away to the west, towards Poole and Wimborne to the east), in cottages with cob walls (a composition of clay and straw), thatched roofs, brick chimney stacks, and gardens. There was a road of far greater antiquity than this one, however, which, in his perambulations, George Loveless would undoubtedly have been aware of.

Ackling Dyke runs in a straight line from north east to south-west, bisecting the Parish of Tolpuddle. Built by the Romans, it ran from Dorchester (Roman name Durnovaria) to Badbury Rings (hill fort), from where it branched, either southwards to Poole on the coast, northwards to Bath (Roman name, 'Aquae Sulis'), or eastwards to Salisbury ('Sorbiodunum'), Silchester

('Calleva Atrebatum' near Reading), and London ('Londinium'). The fact that Ackling Dyke passed just to the west side of the present-day church, indicates that the village may have been important in Roman times – perhaps as a watering place. The parish was far older than this, however.

As he ploughed the northernmost fields of his employer Mrs Susanna Northover's West Farm, George Loveless would have been aware of another historical landmark: an ancient earthwork, known in his time as Weatherby Castle. This had been created during the Iron Age (750 BC to 43 AD), by a people known as the Durotriges, who also produced dark brown or black, burnished pottery, and had a distinctive coinage of their own in the shape of elongated, iron 'currency bars'.[1] Ethnically, the Durotriges were the result of an admixture of the Armorican tribes from the peninsula of that name in Brittany, and the local people of Dorset. Below their hill forts, the countryside was dotted with villages, which were surrounded by, typically, small rectangular fields.[2]

When Roman Emperor Claudius sent four of his legions to cross the Channel and invade Britain in the year 43 AD, the Durotriges put up fierce resistance, but were defeated; a major battle occurring at the Iron Age hill fort of Maiden Castle near Dorchester. Prior to the Durotriges, there were others who left their mark on the landscape.

Neolithic people (of the late Stone Age, 4,500-1,800 BC) built 'henge' (literally, 'hanging rock') monuments consisting of a circular, or oval area delineated by banks and ditches, and enclosing a row of stones or wooden posts. Should Loveless have ventured as far afield as Dorchester, he would have encountered one such edifice, Maumbury Rings, which later became a Roman amphitheatre. It was here that the Dorchester town gallows stood, circa 1700.[3]

Tolpuddle is believed to derive its name from Tola, the wife of Orcus, who owned the land at the time of Canute, King of England from 1016-1035, and also of Denmark and Norway. Orcus, who was one of the King's officers, bequeathed Tolpuddle to the monastery of Abbotsbury, to which institution it continued to belong after the Norman conquest of England in 1066. The second part of the name i.e. 'puddle' (or 'piddle') referred to the river which runs to the south of the village.

What is striking about the various maps and schedules relating to Tolpuddle are the delightful names which attach to the cottages, clusters of cottages, and gardens. For example: 'Snooks Garden'; 'Hooper's Coate'; 'Squibs Coat Tenement' and so forth. As for the fields: several of them bear the name 'Lovelace' (synonymous with Loveless). For example: 'Lovelace's New Place', 'Lovelace's Meadow', and one known simply as 'Lovelace's'. These fields, however, fall within the boundaries, not of West Farm, but of William Brine's East Farm; an indication that other Lovelesses, perhaps kinsmen of George, worked in the area as valued members of the community, and were allocated, or could afford to lease extra land on this account.

This then, was the archetypal Dorset village: aesthetically pleasing to the eye, and set, as it was, in the glorious Dorset countryside. It was a place of sounds: the clatter of horses hooves; the grunting of pigs in the villagers' back yards; the laughter of happy people as they emerged from one of the three ale houses that existed there in former times; the clucking of chickens which were permitted to wander around freely, and the squawking of seagulls as they followed George Loveless's plough. Also of smells: not all of them quite so pleasing, bearing in mind the amount of livestock present! A fine sight it would have been to have seen the cattle being driven to Dorchester Market; or the sheep to the annual fair at Woodbury Hill. However, always lurking behind this pleasing façade were the twin dangers of disease and economic instability, as Loveless and his colleagues had discovered to their cost!

The way in which the economic structure of the village had evolved over the years was as follows. Up until the time of the dissolution of the monasteries in the late 1530s by King Henry VIII, all landowners were, traditionally, obliged to pay monies, or to donate commodities to the Church. These taxes were known as tithes, the patronage (control) of which, within the Manor of Tolpuddle, was in the hands of the Dean and Chapter of Christchurch College Oxford.[4]

In 1536, a safety net was put in place to protect the poor in the form of the Poor Law Act, which meant each parish became responsible for Poor Law administration. From 1572 parishes were obliged to raise monies for the relief of the poor by setting a compulsory rate, and from 1597, every parish was required to appoint overseers (officers for the care) of the Poor.[5]

At the other end of the social scale was the Lord of the Manor; there being two for Tolpuddle in 1544, namely William Riggs and Leonard Brown. As such, they had the right to hold a court, once a year, in order to organise and regulate manorial affairs. Law and order was dispensed at the Quarter Sessions held (as the name implies) four times a year at Dorchester.

In 1662 came the Settlement Law, which enabled a parish, lawfully, to return a newly arrived pauper (a destitute person) to his or her place of origin; this, to prevent such a person from becoming a burden on the rates.

Whatever the economic circumstances, the church could always be sure of its source of income, namely money and goods accruing to it from tithes. This was reflected, in 1775, by the newly arrived Vicar of Tolpuddle, the Reverend Bernard Hodgson, with his lavish expenditure on the vicarage, to which extensive repairs and improvements were made. Hodgson set about replacing the building's thatched roof with a tiled one. He also extended its west end, and built a dairy. Previously a one-storey building, the vicarage now became two-storeys, with additional rooms built into the roof space.

Disease was an ever present danger to those of whatever station in life: notably smallpox in the late 18th century. However, the authorities were not entirely powerless to combat it, as the following extract from the volume, *Particulars Concerning the Village of Tolpuddle* (for September 1791) shows:

> It being found that James Way, aged about 18, had the small pox, the parish held a meeting and agreed that all the poor should be inoculated, who [were] thought proper [suitable] by Mr Kiddle, inoculator of Piddletown (or Puddletown, the adjacent village), or [by] Mr Best of Bere Regis.

Recorded amongst the poor were John and Thomas Lovelace (possibly George's paternal uncles, born 1751 and 1754 respectively; the names Lovelace and Loveless being interchangeable). Four of John's family of five were inoculated by Mr Best; three of Thomas's family of five were inoculated by Mr Kiddle. Incidentally, these inoculations would have been done by introducing cowpox matter from the udder of an infected cow, employing a needle with which to scratch the matter into the skin of the arm - a technique famously pioneered by farmer Benjamin Jesty of Yetminster, Dorset, in the year 1774. (Jesty had observed that milkmaids who caught cowpox from the udders of infected cows, never caught smallpox subsequently). One of the six men of Tolpuddle, James Hammett, was known to have a pock mark over his right cheek bone. This may simply have been the result of an attack of chickenpox, or alternatively of a mild attack of smallpox.[6]

By another Act of Parliament, passed on 3 May 1794, the vicarage tithes of Tolpuddle, 'were commuted [exchanged] for a corn-rent to be paid to the vicar in two half-yearly payments.' The annual corn-rent was:

the price of 397 bushels, 5 gallons, and a half 9 gallon measure of the best wheat, or highest priced wheat that is sold in Oxford Market on two certain days…. The glebe land (that attached to the parish church) allotted to the vicar with what he had before, is in all about 10 acres, 4 of which lie immediately behind the vicarage house.[7]

In the same year, 1794, an Act was passed which would have widespread repercussions for the villagers. The Manor of Tolpuddle was to be enclosed (i.e. common land previously used by the community at large was to be appropriated as private property), and divided into three portions: West Farm (previously Manor Farm); Middle, or Mill Farm; East Farm, this being leased to James Northover. The Act also made provision for, 'industrious cottagers, who might be desirous of adopting the plan, to keep cows,' and to this end, a certain portion of pasture and meadowland was reserved for the purpose; rent being payable by the cottager for each cow pasture which he so utilised. Despite the gloss put on it, the cottagers were now worse off, being charged for something which they had, hitherto, enjoyed for nothing.

In addition, large gardens were allotted to the cottages: the rule being that the cottage was to be let under a so-called 'copyhold' lease (rather than the ordinary leasehold which ran from week to week, or from month to month). This would normally run for the term of one or more stipulated lives.

By such means the landlord is exonerated [i.e. freed from obligation] from the cottages, and the cottager maintains habitation of his own, which he may make as comfortable as he pleases, or has the means of doing, and from which he cannot be removed. In a political point of view, such a measure is highly advantageous, and it gives the poor cottager a property, and consequently a stake and interest in the prosperity of the country.

It was explained that under the terms of the Enclosure Act, which was passed six years before George Loveless was born, it would now be:

In the interest of the proprietors of large manors to discontinue the prevailing and alarming practice of annihilating small leasehold and copyhold estates by throwing them together into large farms, a system too generally prevalent, by which a useful class of yeomanry seems gradually extinguishing [i.e. was being destroyed].[8]

At the turn of the 18th-19th centuries, wages were as follows:

Labourers here [at Tolpuddle] get [at] present, (November 8, 1800), one shilling, for common husbandry work; and the women get sixpence per day; a good, stout lad of about 12 years old gets about sixpence.[9]

1. Mee, Arthur. *The King's England: Dorset*, p.155. 2. Putman, Bill. *The Romans*, p.8.
3.Bridgeman, Major RO. *Historical Notes on Dorchester Prison*.
4.Wirdnam, Audrey. *Pidela: an Account of the Village of Tolpuddle from Early Times*, p.9.
5. Ibid, p.25.
6. *Particulars Concerning the Village of Tolpuddle, 1794*, extract dated 12 September 1791, Dorset History Centre.
7. Hutchins, Reverend John. *The History and Antiquities of the County of Dorset*, Vol.2, p.634.
8. Ibid, p.631.
9. Dorset History Centre. PE TOL IN 3/2.

17

George Loveless and his Family: West Farm

George Loveless's paternal grandfather was John. He married Thomasina Gould, who bore him three (surviving) children: the youngest being Thomas, George's father, christened 3 January 1762. Thomas became a labourer,[1] who married Dinah Stickland, also of Tolpuddle on 4 April 1786; the groom signing his name 'Thomas Lovelass', and the bride writing the letter 'X' (which indicates that she was illiterate). Thomas and Dinah, in their turn, had nine surviving children, of whom George was the sixth. George was born on 2 February 1797, and baptised on 26 February by the vicar, the Reverend Dr Bernard Hodgson, at Tolpuddle's Parish Church of St John the Evangelist.

When, in 1808, the Manor and Estate of Tolpuddle was sold by William Morton Pitt to Samuel Fripp and others, the *Particulars of Sale* list Thomas as a tenant at East Farm - indicating that this was his place of employment.[2] East Farm, 351 acres in size, was farmed by the Northover family, who had arrived in Tolpuddle in late 1795 (the year after the enclosure).[3] Thomas Loveless's wife Dinah died in the year 1809, when their son George was only 12 years old.

On 4 March 1816, Thomas Loveless signed a copyhold lease (based on tenure for a life or a number of lives, as opposed to an ordinary lease, which could be renewed at intervals with the consent of both parties) for a cottage and garden. The property occupied an area of 30 perches (1/5 acre, or approximately 1,000 square yards), for which the annual rental was 15 shillings. The lessors were William Fripp, Esq., and 'another'. The lease was to run for the lives of Thomas himself, then aged 55, and of his sons George aged 18, Samuel 13, and James 8.[4] (The four elder siblings having already left home).[5]

It is interesting to note that when Thomas Loveless signed the above lease for his property, James Northover, farmer at East Farm for whom he worked, was present as a witness. This indicates that Northover valued Thomas as an employee, and supported him in being a copyholder, rather than an ordinary leaseholder, as this would give the latter greater security of tenure of his property.

How could Thomas Loveless have afforded to pay the annual rental of 15 shillings on his property? This is explained by Dorset novelist and poet Thomas Hardy in his article *The Dorsetshire Labourer*:

> If the eldest children of a labourer happened to be girls, then nothing that he can hope to receive for the labour of his one pair of hands, can save him from many hardships... [However,] with a family of strong boys of ages from twelve to seventeen or eighteen, he enjoys a season of prosperity. The very manner of the farmer towards him is deferential; for home-living boys, who in many cases can do men's work at half the wages, and without requiring the perquisites of house, garden-land, and so on, are treasures to the employer of agricultural labour.[6]

It is therefore likely, given the young age at which children commenced work in those days, that Thomas's sons George and Samuel were also employees of James Northover at East Farm, whose wages would have supplemented that of their father Thomas. Also that Thomas's other son James, then aged 8, followed in his sibling's footsteps when he himself attained the age of 12.

James Northover of East Farm was born in 1776. On 10 October 1800, he married Susanna Pont of Fordington, Dorchester.[7] Between 1801 and 1821, Susanna would bear him five (surviving) children, including William and James II. On 2 February 1819, Susanna Northover took out a lease on a, 'dwelling house and premises' at West Farm, previously occupied by farmer,

Tolpuddle, Church and Manor House. Photo: Audrey Wirdnam.

Mr Henry Davis. (The 'dwelling house' was, in fact, the Manor House, which she rented for the sum of 10 shillings per week).[8] (Why the lease was taken out in Susanna's name, rather than that of her husband, is not clear.) In any event, when the Northovers relocated to West Farm, the Lovelesses continued in their employment.[9]

As the name implies, West Farm lay on the west side of the village, adjacent to the church. Previously called Manor Farm, it became West Farm, when in 1794, the Manor of Tolpuddle was enclosed and divided into three portions: the other two farms being East Farm and Mill Farm. West Farm was a substantial one: its fields lying mainly to the west and north side of the village, and including marling pits (marl being a soil consisting of clay and lime with fertilising properties); eweleaze and cowleaze (pastures); a lambing plot; a hopyard (field where hops are grown); a paddock; a spearbed (for the growing of asparagus or broccoli).[10]   Sadly, James Northover's tenure of West Farm was to be a short one, for he died, prematurely, in 1822 at the age of 46, after which his widow Susanna, continued to run the farm.

On 26 December 1824, George Loveless, now aged 26, married Elizabeth Snook of nearby Dewlish. Present at the ceremony, officiated over by The Reverend Thomas Warren, Tolpuddle's vicar (who had succeeded to the living after the death of The Reverend Hodgson in 1805), were Thomas Standfield (later to become George's fellow Martyr) and Samuel Bullen, carpenter.[11]

In 1828, when the Manor and Estate of Tolpuddle were sold by The Reverend Samuel Fripp, 'and others of Bristol', to The Reverend Edward St John of Oakley, Hampshire, it comprised four principal farms: the other three being East Farm (Farmer William Brine); Middle Farm (Farmer Richard Brine); Mill Farm, including the mill (Farmer James Brine). Susanna Northover of West Farm was described as being a, 'Tenant at Will' (one who holds the tenancy for as long a period as the landowner permits) at a rental of £621:11s:6d. per annum.

The 'Particulars, &c' of sale (1828) reveal that West Farm was 577 acres in size, and included a, 'Farmhouse [i.e. the Manor House], Shepherd's house, Cottage, Barns, Buildings, &c... [the] Cottage [being] in the possession of John Lovelace.'[12] This John Loveless (the names Lovelace and Loveless being interchangeable) was not a member of the immediate family (George's elder brother of the same name having moved to West Dorset), and the cottage referred to as being in his possession was probably part of the West Farm complex. Some time in, or after, 1828, Mill Farm and the mill were incorporated into West Farm.[13] Susanna Northover's son James (II) would subsequently become the farmer at West Farm, and his younger brother William, the miller.

George Loveless commenced his working life as an agricultural labourer, and quickly worked his way up to become a husbandman (cultivator of the land). His duties would, therefore, have involved ploughing and sowing: activities which demanded an intimate knowledge of the soil, and of the seasons. His day was a long one, especially in the summer months, when every hour of light was precious.

The first Monday following the Twelfth Day of Christmas was known as Plough Monday, when preparation of the soil, prior to the planting of the spring corn and other crops, began. Ploughing enabled surface weeds and the remains of previous crops to decay and return their nutrients to the soil, where wind, rains, and frost would render its texture soft and crumbly, and therefore more receptive to the newly planted seeds. Ploughing was also important for aeration and drainage.

The horses at West Farm were traditionally, harnessed to the plough, side by side. Carthorses were used, rather than the larger shire horses, which although immensely powerful, were unwieldy and expensive to maintain. Instead of a bridle, trace chains ran on either side of each horse and all the way back to the ploughman. A wooden 'spreader' was positioned at the rear to keep them clear of the horses' flanks. As the horses knew what was required of them, these trace chains only came into play when they reached the end of the furrow and had to be turned around.

Many qualities were required of the ploughman including: the ability to adjust the depth of his ploughshare to best advantage; a good rapport with the horses under his control; the ability to work with the prevailing weather, rather than to attempt to oppose it. An experienced ploughman, such as George Loveless, could plough an acre of land in 8 hours, allowing for rest periods. And, of course, whilst he was performing the semi-automatic functions of ploughing and sowing, he would have had plenty of time to think!

❖ ❖ ❖

As for George Loveless's eight siblings, John, the eldest, became apprenticed as flax dresser to a Mr John Clay of Burton Bradstock and spent the rest of his life in West Dorset.[14] (It will be remembered that it was John who had advised George when he created the Tolpuddle union.)[15] Dianne, as already stated, married George's fellow martyr, Thomas Standfield. William followed in John's footsteps, and also moved to West Dorset, where he too became a flax dresser.[16] Robert moved to London, where he also worked as a flax dresser. (A clue that Robert, too, may have helped his brother George in the latter's union activities is to be found in a statement made, years later, by George, to Thomas Mason, Assistant Police Magistrate of Hobart, Tasmania, that it was his 'relation' George avoided using the term 'brother'. Robert, who had assisted him in forming the Friendly Society – [union].)[17] Samuel moved to the Channel Island of Jersey, where he worked as a labourer.[18] As for Susanna and Thomas, their fate is not known.

As already mentioned, James, like George, became a Methodist preacher; joined the Tolpuddle union, and worked for Mrs Northover at West Farm. In 1830, he married Sarah Daniel. At the time of his trial in 1834, the couple had two children: Eli Wesley and Emily, and Sarah was pregnant with another, Theophilus.

1.Inventory of the properties and villagers of Tolpuddle, 1776 and 1804, Dorset History Centre, PE/TOL:IN3/2.
2. Dorset History Centre, D1 11316.
3. Hodgson, Reverend Dr Bernard, Vicar of Tolpuddle. *Inventory of Inhabitants 1795* - provided by him at the bishop's request - included the entry, 'Northover and family not yet come', Dorset History Centre, PE/TOL: IN3/2:
4. Tolpuddle Manor, Particulars of Sale 1808, Dorset History Centre, D396/T762.
5. *Schedule for the Manor of Tolpuddle* for 1830 reveals that Thomas and his sons were still in occupation of the cottage at that time, Dorset History Centre, D1 11359.
6. Hardy, Thomas. *The Dorsetshire Labourer*.
7. Fordington, Dorset. Bishop's Transcripts.
8. *Schedule for the Manor of Tolpuddle*, Dorset History Centre, D COO M1.
9. *Hansard Parliamentary Debates*, Thomas Wakley, House of Commons, 25 June 1835.
10. Tolpuddle: Tithe Apportionment 1840, and Tithe Map 1843, Dorset History Centre, T/TOL.
11. Dorset History Centre, PE/TOL; RE3/3.
12. Particulars &c. of Sale of the Manor of Tolpuddle 1828, Dorset History Centre, D/KAT/E11.
13. Tolpuddle: Tithe Apportionment for 1840 and Tithe Map of 1843, Dorset History Centre, DHC T/TOL.

14. On 23 April 1812, John Loveless married Ann Mary Way born Up Lyme, Devon, the groom again signing his name, and the bride writing an 'X' as her mark. Bealing Papers: Settlement Order 1859, Dorset History Centre, D 1083.

15. Citrine, Walter (Editor). *The Book of the Martyrs of Tolpuddle, 1834-1934*, p.236. 1841 Census, shows John Loveless living at Burton Bradstock, with his wife Mary and their children William 15, an apprentice shoemaker; Robert 12; Sarah 7, and George 4.

16. William moved first to Bradpole, and later to Burton Bradstock. 1841 Dorset Census, Burton Bradstock.

17. George Loveless to Thomas Mason, 15 September 1834. Public Record Office, CO 280/52.

18. Here, Samuel married, and had a daughter Mary Ann. 1851 Census, Jersey.

The Martyrs: Who Lived Where?

It is surprising, considering that the name Loveless is, today, known throughout the world, and particularly in trade union circles, that nobody, until now, has been able to ascertain, precisely, *where* in the village of Tolpuddle the Loveless family lived (bearing in mind, that as copyholders since March 1816, they continued to occupy the same property, even after George and James had been arrested, tried, and transported to Australia).

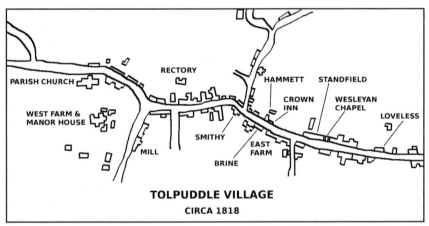

Tolpuddle, Plan of The Village, circa 1818.

On 27 January 1934, a Mrs Hammett (believed to be Mary Hammett, a niece of James Hammett,[1] who was currently living in a cottage at Church Hill, Tolpuddle), recorded in a 'Memorandum of Interview' that she, 'thought it [the Loveless's cottage] had stood on the further side (away from Dorchester) of the old [Wesleyan] chapel.' She also stated that the cottage, 'was now pulled down.'[2]

A month previously, on 31 December 1933, Frank Hammett - who was related to both the Hammett and Loveless families,[3] had written to Walter M Citrine, General Secretary of the Trade Union Congress, saying, in respect of where the

Loveless family might have lived, 'I think I have heard my mother say it was the cottage occupied in my boyhood days by Thomas Cross, situated on the left-hand side after passing the village well.'[4] (This well, the remains of which are visible today, was situated 10 yards or so back from the main road on its south side).[5] The cottage referred to was, therefore, on the north side of the road.

Tolpuddle's Tithe Apportionment of 1840, and its corresponding Tithe Map of 1843, indicates that the Cross family did, indeed, occupy a cottage in the village. It stood on Plot No. 97, the landowner of which was William Cross, and the occupiers Richard Cross, labourer, and others. (By 1840, this cottage had been converted into three tenements).

It is also possible, from the 1840 Tithe Map, to calculate that the size of Plot No. 97 was almost exactly 30 perches – 1/5 acre. (This, by extrapolation from the plot opposite, whose area is specified on the map in acres, roods, and perches). This again correlates with the lease agreement, signed by Thomas Loveless in 1816, in which the area of ground of the cottage and garden is recorded as being 30 perches. Also, none of the other plots in any way approximate to these dimensions.

Was Mrs Hammett correct in stating that the Loveless's cottage had been demolished? From the 1843 Tithe Map, it is possible to calculate the proportionate distances between Whitehill Lane, East Farm, and the 'Cross' family cottage on Plot No. 97. The distance from Whitehill Lane to the western end of East Farm House is 88 paces. From the Tithe Map, the expected distance from East Farm House to the 'Cross' family cottage is 200 paces.

Pacing out the distances brings a great surprise. There is, indeed, a property at the place in question – so-called 'Pixies Cottage' – an ancient, Listed (protected) Building. It is, therefore, proved,

Tolpuddle, George Loveless's Cottage, circa 1900.
Photo: Audrey Wirdnam

beyond reasonable doubt, that this was where the Loveless family lived, and that Mrs Hammett was mistaken in believing that their cottage had been pulled down.

What of the other four Martyrs? Where in the village did they live?

Thomas Robert and John Standfield
Of all the Martyr families, that of the Standfields was, traditionally, by far the most affluent: their family home being a property (formerly known as Wills's Cottage), situated on the north side of the main street, just to the east of the Crown Inn. Here, the Standfields had lived for at least five generations.

Tolpuddle, Thomas Standfield's cottage.

Most affluent of all was Martyr Thomas's paternal great grandfather Robert (I), a carpenter married to Katharine, who owned, not only his house (which was leasehold), but also a timber yard, working shops, outhouses, another house called 'Clarks', and a booth (hut or temporary dwelling) at Woodbury Hill. This booth, according to his will, contained eight bedsteads, and may have been for the use of visitors to the famous annual Woodbury Fair. Robert I's affluence is attested to by the inventory of his possessions, which included: three Delph (as in Delftware) pots; a decanter and a glass salt; two Delft punchbowls; three feather beds; three coats; three flannel waistcoats; three pairs of breeches; two hats; two wigs; two pairs of shoes; seven pairs of stockings; eight shirts; three handkerchiefs; a pair of silver shoe buckles; horses in the cellars; sixteen hogs heads of strong beer in a cask, and a new waggon.

Martyr Thomas's father, also Robert (II), appears in the 1808 *Particulars of Sale* for Tolpuddle Manor as being the copyhold leaseholder of a cottage and garden attached to James Northover's East Farm (where, at that time, it is probable that George Loveless, together with his brother and father, were also employed). Robert II, described by The Reverend Dr Bernard Hodgson in his village survey of 1804, as a farmer,[6] also rented 94 acres at Mill Farm, for which he paid an annual tithe of 37 bushels and 4 gallons of corn. Robert II married Elizabeth Baker. The couple had eight surviving children, of whom Martyr Thomas, born 11 November 1789, was the second.

Martyr Thomas married George Loveless's sister Diana in 1812 and the couple had seven children, of whom (Martyr) John, born 1813, was the first. The fact that both Thomas and John became employees of Mrs Northover at West Farm, rather than farmers in their own right, is an indication that their fortunes were on the decline.

James Hammett
Martyr James Hammett was baptised on 3 May 1812. His parents were John and Elizabeth, The Reverend Hodgson's 1804 survey of Tolpuddle recording that John was a bricklayer.

A letter survives, written by William Rogers Loveless (no doubt a kinsman of George Loveless) and dated 15 May 1934 (i.e. 100 years after the trial and conviction of the Martyrs) to Mr Walter M Citrine, General Secretary of the Trade Union Congress. It refers to the fact that James Hammett was arrested (prior to his trial in 1834), 'at cottages in the rear of the Crown Inn...', and included with it is a sketch plan, made by him, of these two semi-detached cottages. The Hammett family was a large one, James having eight siblings in all. So it is quite feasible that they occupied both the cottages, which were known as Drew's Tenements, and

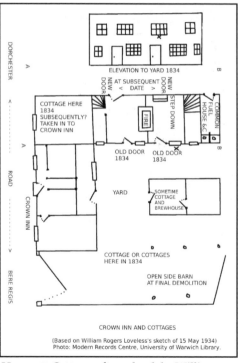

Hammett Cottages, from sketch by William Rogers Loveless, courtesy Warwick University Modern Records Centre.

owned (not leased) by John Bullen, landlord of the Crown Inn.

WR Loveless states that both James Hammett and his younger brother John lived in the cottage as boys. He also mentions that when the cottages were demolished, he asked if he might have the window board from the top left window of the right hand cottage as it faced the yard (see plan) into which James Hammett had carved his initials. (This relic still exists, and is currently in the keeping of the Martyrs Museum at Tolpuddle). Says WR Loveless:

> James Hammett was closely associated with these cottages during a very large portion of his life, both before and after transportation.[7]

James Brine
The youngest of the Martyrs, James Brine, was baptised on 31 January 1813, the son of shoemaker John and his wife Catherine. When John died in 1829, his wife was left on her own to bring up her six children - three sons (Charles, James [the Martyr], and Joseph), and three daughters (Mary, Anna, and Jane). (Charles, also a shoemaker, was aged 19 when his father died, and he now became the breadwinner).[8]

William Puckett of Dorchester (a relation of the Hammetts), writing on 15 January 1934, to Walter Citrine of the TUC, stated that, 'the cottage in which James Brine lived... is directly opposite the present Public House [i.e. The Martyrs' Inn, The Crown having burned down early in the 20th century]'.[9] This statement is borne out by the Tolpuddle's Tithe Apportionment (1840) and Tithe Map (1843), which indicates that this cottage (Plot 113, with garden and orchard) was occupied by Martyr James Brine's elder brother Charles (the landowner being James Brine, farmer of East Farm).

1. Family tree supplied by Tolpuddle Martyrs Museum, Tolpuddle, Dorset.
2. University of Warwick, Modern Record Centre, *Memorandum of Interview*, dated 27 January 1934, Present, Mrs Hammett and Mr Wray, Mss. JW/EG/612.
3. Frank Hammett's father was cousin to James Hammett, and his mother was cousin to George Loveless.
4. University of Warwick, Modern Record Centre, Mss. 292/1/1.91/8.
5. Information supplied by Mrs Beth King of East Farm.
6. Dorset History Centre, PE/TOL;IN3/2.
7. University of Warwick, Modern Records Centre, MSS.292/1.91/16.
8. Census, Tolpuddle, 1841.
9. William Puckett to Walter M Citrine, 15 January 1934, University of Warwick, Modern Record Centre, Mss. 292/1.91/8.

19

How Methodism came to Tolpuddle

George Loveless's father Thomas, his mother Dinah, he himself, and all his siblings were christened at Tolpuddle's Anglican (Church of England) Parish Church of St John the Evangelist, which is where George was subsequently married by The Vicar of Tolpuddle, the Reverend Thomas Warren. When members of the Loveless family first became interested in Methodism is not clear. However, it was in 1810 that a 'Dissenter's Licence' (licence which legitimised a premises for use as a meeting house) was first granted, 'for the dwelling place of Thomas Loveless.'[1] The inference is, therefore, that George, his brother James, and their other siblings, were first guided towards Methodism by their father. (The house of Thomas Standfield was also a venue for their meetings).

John and Charles Wesley
Thomas Loveless, born in 1762, was a contemporary of John Wesley (born 1703) and his brother Charles (born 1707), the founders of Methodism. He may possibly have heard one or other of them preach; if not, then he would certainly have been aware of them by reputation.

The Wesley family had connections with Dorset, in that Great Grandfather Bartholomew Westley (an early spelling of the name), was Rector of Charmouth. Batholomew's son, Grandfather John Westley - although never formally ordained into the ministry - became a non-conformist teacher (one who does not conform to the established church), and in 1662 he was arrested on this account, under the Act of Uniformity of 1560 (which declared Anglicanism to be the national religion, and which repudiated the authority of the Pope of Rome).[2] As will be seen, this tendency to dissent was one which ran in the family! John and Charles's father Samuel Wesley was ordained priest in 1689, and in 1695, became Rector of Epworth in Lincolnshire. Here, John and Charles were born; their mother being Susanna (née Annesley), who had a total of ten surviving children.

John Wesley graduated from Christ Church College, Oxford, and was ordained priest in 1728. His younger brother Charles followed in his footsteps, and whilst at Christ Church, founded with fellow undergraduates a religious society known as 'The Holy Club'; the young men who made up its membership being known as Methodists - the word dating back, originally, to a first century school of medicine. They were bound by strict principles of piety and morality, and by equally strict rules in respect of fasting and prayer. In 1729, John joined Charles's 'Holy Club', and became its leader.[3]

In 1735, John Wesley travelled to the newly established British colony of Georgia in North America, as pastor to its first settlers in Savannah. In this, he was assisted by Charles, who was ordained priest in the same year. Although the visit was not a success, it brought John into contact with the Moravians, a Protestant sect whose simple faith he admired. Immigrants from Moravia (now the Czech Republic) had founded the sect in Saxony in the early eighteenth century and had then emigrated to America.

In 1739, John Wesley set about creating a 'New Room' at Bristol; this to be a base for his itinerant ministry to the west and south west of England. He now commenced, what was to be, a lifetime of 'field [open air] preaching', in which he delivered an estimated 40,000 sermons, and travelled many thousands of miles - mainly on horseback - to bring his message to the flock. He and his brother also produced a large collection of psalms and hymns.

Although John Wesley was anxious to remain a member of the Church of England, his famous comment, 'I look upon all the world as my parish,'[4] was hardly likely to endear him to the latter institution, which regarded Methodism as dissenting religion, and the members of the Methodist Church as Dissenters (those who have separated themselves from the Established Church). In any event, Wesley's wish became impossible, when in 1784, following the American War of Independence, he committed an act of schism (breach), by ordaining two of his ministers to serve his American congregations.

During the years 1725-90, John Wesley kept a journal, at the beginning of which he included an introductory letter. In it, he posed the following rhetorical questions:

1. Whether it does not concern all men of all conditions to imitate Him [Jesus Christ], as much as they can, 'who went about doing good'? Whether we can be happy at all hereafter, unless we have, according to our power, 'fed the hungry, clothed the naked, visited those that are sick, and in prison'; and made all these actions

subservient to a higher purpose, even the saving of souls from death?

2. Whether, upon these considerations, we may not try to do good to our acquaintance[s]? Particularly, whether we may not try to convince them of the necessity of being Christians? Whether of the consequent necessity of being scholars? Whether of the necessity of method and industry, in order to either learning or virtue? Whether we may not try to persuade them to confirm and increase their industry, by communicating as often as they can? Whether we may not mention to them the authors whom we conceive to have wrote the best on those subjects?

3. Whether we may not give them… ['necessitous' families – i.e. families in need], if they can read, a Bible, Common-Prayer Book, or Whole Duty of Man? [*The Whole Duty of Man According to the Law of Nature* (1673) was written by German writer Samuel Pufendorf. It argues that the basis of natural law lies in the need for man to cultivate sociability. The fact that George Loveless was familiar with such a work indicates the breadth of his reading.] Whether we may not enforce upon them, more especially, the necessity of private prayer, and of frequenting the church and sacrament? Whether we may not contribute, what little we are able, toward having their children clothed and taught to read? Whether we may not take care that they be taught their catechism [compendium of teachings], and short prayers for morning and evening?

From this, it can be seen, that whereas Anglicanism was principally concerned, in those days, with worship, prayer, and maintaining the status quo, Methodism was essentially a hands-on religion, which emphasised not only evangelism, but personal responsibility, not only for one's self in respect of piety, self-discipline, industriousness, and study, but also for one's fellows who were to be supported in times of need and sickness.

Methodism in Dorset
Methodism came to Dorset when stonemason William Nelson arrived at Portland (a peninsula stretching 5 miles out to sea, south of the coastal town of Weymouth) in 1743, and become leader of Dorset's first Methodist congregation. In 1746, Nelson received a visit from Charles Wesley, who preached, on 6 June of that year, 'to a houseful of staring, loving people….'[5] When Nelson died in 1770, Methodism waned in Portland until the chance

arrival, in 1793, of Robert Carr Brackenbury esquire of Raithby Hall, Lincolnshire, to whom John Wesley had given a special, roving commission to preach at Methodist meeting houses.[6]

Not only did Brackenbury preach to the people of Portland, but in 1792, he built them a chapel at his own expense.[7] Soon, through his efforts, and those of his assistant George Smith, further Methodist meeting houses were established, not only on the Isle of Portland, but also on the mainland, at such places as Dorchester and Weymouth.

Charles Wesley's elder brother John first ventured into South Dorset in 1774, where he preached at Corfe Castle and at Langton Matravers in the Isle of Purbeck. In 1776, he revisited Purbeck and preached again at Corfe Castle, and afterwards at Melcombe Regis. A favourite place was Shaftesbury in north Dorset, where he preached no less than sixteen times between July 1750 and August 1785.

Organisation of the Methodist Church

Methodism evolved from societies created in towns and villages, where meetings were held in private houses, or in other suitable accommodation. When a society had grown to such a size that its members were able to afford it, they would build their own chapel.

By the year 1746, John Wesley had divided the country into seven circuits, each comprising a number of societies under the supervision of a full-time itinerant preacher, who usually remained in post for a period of two years. Each circuit covered a large area, the County of Dorset being on the Bristol Circuit, as was Somerset, Wiltshire, Oxfordshire, and Gloucestershire. The preacher would travel on horseback, with saddlebags containing, 'spare clothes, some of his personal library, and a stock of Wesley's publications for sale. In winter [when snow lay on the ground] he sometimes added a spade.'[8]

In the early days, preachers were maintained by the Methodist families whom they visited. From 1752, they were awarded an allowance of £12 per annum, which in 1769 was increased by £10 per annum for a married man. By 1800 the basic rate had been increased to £16 per annum. A preacher was permitted to drink beer or ale, but spirits were frowned upon, and the 1795 Methodist Conference (Church's supreme legislative body) banned the smoking of tobacco altogether.[9]

By the mid-nineteenth century, Dorset's Bristol-based Wesleyan circuit had been subdivided into seven smaller ones centred at: Poole/Wareham; Weymouth; Shaftesbury; Sherborne; Dorchester; Bridport; Wimborne. In 1831, the Weymouth circuit was further divided, and the village of Tolpuddle, previously on the Weymouth circuit, now came within the Dorchester Circuit.[10]

The Tolpuddle Chapel

Tolpuddle's first Wesleyan chapel was erected in 1818, on a plot of land immediately adjacent to the Standfield family home on its east side. The property, however, was not owned by the Methodist Church. Instead, under the terms of a lease drawn up in September 1818, Robert Standfield, a man of substance, would let a plot of land adjacent to his house which he owned to his son (Martyr) Thomas, on a copyhold basis (i.e. for the period of one or more lives).

The three 'lifeholders', whose names appeared on the lease, included Thomas Standfield, together with Mrs Mary Butler of Woodbury, Devonshire, and Mrs Ann Fitzherbert of Chideock, Dorset. These ladies were sisters, their father being The Reverend Gilbert Langdon, Vicar of Milton Abbas in mid-Dorset.[11] How had this come about, given the animosity that existed between the Anglican and Methodist churches? The full story will probably never be known. However, Thomas and the two sisters were of a

Tolpuddle, Wesleyan Chapel of 1818 (now in disrepair). Photo: Audrey Wirdnam.

similar social standing, and may well have come into contact with each other on this account. Also, there was a local connection in that Ann Fitzherbert's (née Langdon) first marriage had been to John Warren Plowman, whose father John became curate of Tolpuddle in 1764 and was subsequently appointed its vicar.

The chapel was originally a single-storied building with a thatched roof. Its walls were built of cob, set on a brick plinth and decorated with flint course. It measured some 20 feet by 30 feet, and would have been entered from the street by way of the doorway at the (short) south wall. At the opposite end, beneath the lancet window set into the gable, was the pulpit, probably single-decker in design, on account of the lack of available height. In front of the pulpit was the communion table, surrounded by a rail. Box pews were provided for the chapel's elders, and bench pews for the congregation.[12]

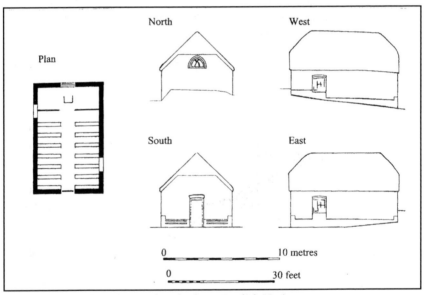

Tolpuddle, Plan of Wesleyan Chapel. Photo: English Heritage.

George Loveless was involved in the project from the very beginning, being one of the chapel's twelve trustees. The others were Thomas Standfield and James Sansom - labourers from Tolpuddle; John Chapman - labourer from Tincleton; a confectioner; a maltster; a blacksmith from Weymouth; another maltster from Broadmayne; a farmer from the Isle of Purbeck; a draper from

Wareham; a cordwainer (leather worker) from Winterborne Kingston, and a carpenter from Anderson. William Worth was designated as Superintendent Preacher.[13]

The trustees were bound by John Wesley's Deed Poll (or 'Deed of Declaration'), executed by him in March 1784, in order to define the identity, constitution, and powers of the Methodist Conference after his death.[14] Rules were also laid down:

> ...for the annual meetings, procedure, records, and officers of the Conference... [which] had the right to admit preachers on trial, to receive them into full connexion [Methodist circle], and expel them when necessary.[15]

However, as George knew well, to embrace Methodism was to court unpopularity. 'I am, from principle, a Dissenter,' he said, 'and by some, in Tolpuddle, it is considered as the sin of witchcraft.' If anyone is in doubt as to the degree of persecution suffered by the Methodists of Tolpuddle, they have only to refer to an article which appeared in the Salisbury Journal, dated 19 October 1818:

> On Tuesday last, a Methodist Chapel was opened in the village of Tolpuddle. Dorset, and a number of persons accompanied the Ministers from Weymouth on the occasion. During the evening Service, when the chapel was much crowded, some little disturbance was made on the outside, but peace was soon restored. About 8 o'clock, when the Ministers and their friends were preparing to return, a mob of about 100 persons were found assembled near a chaise and another carriage, which were in attendance to convey them. These persons behaved in a most turbulent manner. A lady belonging to the Minister's party, before she could get into the chaise, was pushed down a bank into the road; the horses were much frightened by the tumult and noise, and the driver was, for a considerable time unable to proceed. The ladies were under the necessity of walking a great distance, exposed to the most brutal insults. For more than two miles, in a very bad road, the drivers, horses, and carriages, were pelted by the mob, with stones, mud, &c.; the windows of the chaise were broken, and even the side of the chaise was pierced by a stone; one lady who rode by the side of the driver had a severe blow on her head; and at Piddle Town, two miles

from Tolpuddle, the driver received a blow in his neck, of which he is now confined, and which, had it not been for a large neck-cloth, would probably have proved fatal. Mr. Bailey, of the Golden Lion, Weymouth, to whom the chaise belongs, has offered five guineas reward for a discovery of the offenders.[16]

The 'Plan for the Wesleyan preachers in the Weymouth Circuit [of which Tolpuddle was then a part] on the Lord's Day [Sunday] 1829 – 1830', indicates that preachers were not confined to their own Circuits. In the right-hand column were listed the names of the accredited Wesleyan Methodist preachers, twenty-seven in all (two of whom were 'on trial'). They included: 'J Loveless' (probably George's younger brother James, Preacher No.24); 'W Loveless' (probably George's older brother William, No.25), and simply 'Loveless' (presumably George himself, No.8). In the left-hand column was the list of the nineteen towns and villages which they visited, stretching east, to Ower on the shores of Poole Harbour; north, as far as Dewlish; south, to the Isle of Portland. For every single Sunday of the month, a named preacher was in attendance. For example, on 29 November 1829, George Loveless was to be found preaching at [Winterbourne] Houghton, taking his text from the book of Isaiah 1, and John 21.[17]

It comes as a surprise to some, that George Loveless, a man of humble origins, was not only erudite, but highly literate. The first quality was due to his natural ability. The second was a reflection of the Methodist belief in education and scholarship. Not only were members and preachers alike expected to be able to read and write, the Methodist Church also provided the wherewithal for them to do so. For example, George Loveless, an authority on the *Holy Bible*, who was also acquainted with the works of other writers such as the English poets John Milton and Edward Young, was known to possess a modest collection of theological books.[18]

For George Loveless, a thinking man with a highly developed sense of what was right and of what was wrong, the appeal of Methodism was obvious. Here was a religion which advocated industriousness, soberness, the worth of each and every person as an individual, and the belief in a duty of care for other human beings. The Anglican Church, on the other hand, was perceived as being at best apathetic, and at worst hostile, towards working people. In fact the behaviour of The Reverend Warren, Vicar of Tolpuddle, made Loveless suspect that the institution was actually complicit in creating the circumstances which had, prior to his arrest and trial, made unbearable the lives of himself and his fellow workers and their families. One day, the time would come when George Loveless would have the opportunity to portray the Anglican Church in its true light. In the meantime, he had many hardships to suffer.

For the Lovelesses and for the Standfields, their dedication to Methodism was beyond doubt. As for fellow Martyr James Brine, he became a convert to Methodism only later in his life, and James Hammett probably not at all.

Was there a connection between Methodism and trade unionism? The answer is, yes, in particular with regard to the so-called Primitive Methodists (a movement which originated in Staffordshire in 1811), who regarded their organisation as less centralised and more democratic than the so-called Wesleyan Methodists. Whether the Tolpuddle Methodists regarded themselves as 'Primitive' is not known, but they clearly embraced the Primitive philosophy.

Many Primitive Methodists went on to become trade union leaders, and it is not difficult to imagine how the natural progression from Methodism to trade unionism came about, since to the mind of the Methodist preacher, there was inherent hypocrisy in catering for the spiritual needs of the flock if that flock's material requirements were ignored and disregarded.

1. *Dorchester Methodist Circuit in the 19th century*, information supplied by Lloyd N Thomas, Circuit Archivist, Dorchester, p.29.
2. Simon, John S. *Methodism in Dorset*, p.64.
3. Vicars, John A. *A Dictionary of Methodism in Britain and Ireland*, p.230.
4. Wesley, John. *Journal*, 11 June 1739.
5. Biggs, Barry J. *The Wesleys and the Early Dorset Methodists*, p.23.
6. Ibid, p.28.
7. Ibid, p.27.
8. Ibid, p.5.
9. Ibid, p.5.
10. Dorset History Centre, NM9:C1/RE1/1.
11. *Dorchester Methodist Circuit in the 19th century*, op.cit., p.29.
12.*Architectural History* (2001), Vol.4, pp.275-282, by David M Robinson.
13.*Dorchester Methodist Circuit in the 19th century*, op.cit., p.30.
14.Vicars, John A. *A Dictionary of Methodism in Britain and Ireland*. p.92.
15.Ibid, p.92.
16.*Salisbury and Winchester Journal*, 19 October 1818.
17. Dorset History Centre, HS NM2:S19 MS 1/1.
18.*Hansard Parliamentary Debates,* Thomas Wakley, House of Commons, 25 June 1835.

20

A Howl of Protest: Thomas Wakley

Within a week of the conviction of the Six Men of Dorset on 19 March 1834, a public meeting was held at the National Institution, Charlotte Street, London, in order that measures should be taken to obtain the remission of what were described as the, 'extraordinary sentences passed at the Dorchester Assizes....' The number of people in attendance at this meeting was estimated to be in excess of 10,000.[1]

On 26 March 1834, Mr William Hughes Hughes, an Independent and a Reformist (one in favour of extending suffrage), who would be elected M.P. for Oxford the following year, told the House of Commons that he had been, 'charged to present a petition bearing the signatures of 1,563 of his constituents: inhabitants and house-holders of the city of Oxford...' which declared that the sentence passed on the men was, 'too rigorous and too severe', and that it should therefore be 'softened'.[2]

Parliamentary reaction was mixed: the majority of members choosing to side with the authorities, rather than with the six men. However, the Right Honourable Craven Fitz Hardinge Berkeley, M.P. for Cheltenham, also an Independent and a Reformist, presented a petition from the inhabitants of his constituency, 'praying that the House would present an Address to his Majesty, to mitigate the punishment of the Dorchester agriculturists for administering unlawful oaths.'[3] Four days later, Joseph Hume, M.P. for Middlesex (who had been active in having the Combination Acts of 1824 repealed), enquired as to what grounds had led the government to act in this case? Hume could attribute the government's action, 'to nothing but a cowardly feeling on its part, which finding the trade unions opposed to its views, was anxious to get at them, and had seized the first victims it could.'[4]

On 19 April 1834, Radical newspaper *The True Sun* disclosed that a meeting was to take place two days later at Copenhagen Fields, near Kings Cross, London, of, 'members of the trade unions resident in the metropolis and its vicinity.' Members would then proceed *en masse* to Whitehall, there to hand over to the Secretary of State a petition to the King, 'praying a remission of the sentence passed on the six men convicted at Dorchester.'

The event duly took place, and was a greater success than anyone could have imagined. Said *The True Sun*:

> At half past seven [a.m.] about five and thirty banners, fixed to long poles, formed of crimson and blue cotton, each bearing the initials of the different lodges of trades, were arranged in a line along the side of the road... Before eight o'clock, the lodges, preceded by their respective officers, decorated with different insignia and all wearing crimson ribbons, commenced marching on the ground, five and six abreast, with great regularity and almost military precision...
>
> It was not until half past nine, that the committee was able to instruct the procession to move off, by which time other lodges had joined them, 'from all parts of the compass.' The 'dense mass' of supporters who also joined them and assembled behind the banners was, 'almost incalculable', and, 'the intended line of march' appeared to be, 'perfectly black with human beings, who stood in thousands on the raised mounds on each side.'

In fact, it was *The True Sun*'s reporter's opinion that this assembly, 'certainly far exceeded in numerical strength and regularity of movement anything of the same sort ever previously witnessed....'[5] Not only that, but, 'the shops along the whole line of the route were closed and business appeared to be completely suspended,' and as the procession proceeded, it was, 'not unfrequently greeted by loud cheers from the congregated spectators lining the streets....'[6]

Of the trades represented, the most numerous were the tailors, who, 'were distinguishable by a certain jauntiness of carriage, which together with a due exercise of their art in personal adornment, somewhat covered a lack of thewes [muscles] and sinews.' In contrast, there were brawny blacksmiths and metal-workers, 'excavators, rough in garb and formidable as to bodily strength... coal-heavers' attired in their 'leather fantails' (a particular type of hat which they wore), who, 'alone of the separate bodies manifested a turn for the boisterous.'[7]

111

The True Sun's reporter observed several Members of Parliament from both Houses amongst the crowd:

> ...witnessing with astonishment the peaceable conduct of the unionists' from many parts. As they proceeded there was dead silence and nothing was heard but the tramping of feet. Persons of intelligence who witnessed the long black silent and unbroken stream of human beings... acclaimed, 'This is not a common procession of petitioners, but a nation in movement.'[8]

Finally, a delegation of five unionists carried the 'monster petition' into the Home Office, where they were met by Lord Melbourne's secretary Mr JM Phillips, whose response was predictably begrudging. He informed the unionists, that although Lord Melbourne was in the office, he was unable to receive a petition presented under such circumstances, and in such a manner. However, His Lordship had seen a copy of the petition, and did not disapprove of the language of it. If it were to be presented on another day, and in a becoming manner, he would receive it and lay it before the King.[9]

In its edition of 26 April 1834, *The Pioneer* declared exuberantly, 'Last Monday was a day in Britain's history which long will be remembered; for labour put its hat upon its head and walked towards the throne.'[10]

The following summer, on 25 June 1835, Lord John Russell, who had become Home Secretary the previous April, addressed the House of Commons on the subject of a Motion to be put before it by Mr Thomas Wakley, Member of Parliament for Finsbury, London, since 1835 (a Radical who bore no allegiance to either of the main political parties), for an address to be made to his Majesty the King for the granting of pardon to the Dorchester labourers, and for an order for their recall to England.

Lord Russell declared that he had given much attention to the case of the Dorchester labourers, and considered it his duty to recommend to the Crown the following course of action. All six men were to be granted a pardon, provided that they remained in the colonies. If, after two years from their arrival in Australia, they had been of good conduct, then four of them were to be granted a full pardon and allowed to return to England. In the case of, 'those persons named Loveless' – i.e. George and James – 'whom he considered the most culpable, and who, in fact, had incited the others to the commission of the offence,' they would not be allowed to return to England. In regard to these two men, he considered that if he were to recommend the Crown, 'to extend further mercy to them, he should be lending himself to weaken the authority of the law, and to impair the influence which that great institution, trial by judge and jury, ought to have in this country.'

In reply, Wakley said, that if the proposal had been to treat all six men in the same way, then he would have been satisfied. However, he was prepared to prove that the two men were innocent, and should not, in fact, have been prosecuted at all. Now came an in-depth speech by Wakley, who had taken the trouble to visit Elizabeth, George Loveless's wife, in person, in order to ascertain what her circumstances were. He had also received a letter from Loveless himself.

Wakley told the House that it was common knowledge that trade unions had been instituted in London in July 1833, 4 months prior to the creation of a union at Tolpuddle. Despite the fact that the membership of the London unions was numbered in hundreds, the government, by omitting to interfere with, let alone to prosecute them, had, 'by acquiescence, at least,' given sanction to them.

Wakley also pointed out that, 'a placard containing extracts from certain Acts of Parliament relating to unions was found in the pocket of one of the men [George Loveless]. These extracts, which constituted the magistrates 'Caution', did not mention a specific Act by name. Loveless obtained possession of it only on the Sunday prior to the day on which he had been taken into custody. In other words, Loveless had obtained, 'cognisance of the nature of his offence (if he had committed any) only after the offence had been perpetrated.' Wakley assured the House that the men of Tolpuddle, 'were actually going to break up [i.e. disband] the Union in consequence of seeing that paper,' but that they had not had the time to do so.

Wakley complained that the chief witness for the prosecution (Edward Legg) had been imprisoned in order for his testimony to be secured. Furthermore, the fact that this witness was, 'in the employment of that very magistrate who caused the labourers to be apprehended' (i.e. James Frampton) made it appear that, 'the whole matter' was a, 'conspiracy to entrap the accused.'

Wakley now turned to the Act of Parliament upon which the men had been convicted. If the men had been indicted under the Act 39 Geo. III (1799 'Combination Act'), which was:

> ...avowedly framed for the purpose of putting down all secret associations, with the exception of the society of freemasons, and two or three other societies therein specifically named... [then] the poor fellows [i.e. the six men] might then have been proceeded against summarily before the magistrate, and been committed to prison for three months for taking an oath not required or authorised by law.

However, by electing to try the men under the Act 37 Geo. III, ('Mutiny Act'), the judge had the power, on their conviction, to transport them for the term of seven years.

Wakley admitted, that whereas it was true that the Tolpuddle union society was a secret one, nevertheless he denied that it was an illegal combination. The Act of 1826, 'sec. 4, Geo. 4th, cap.129' (Repeal of the Combination Acts), an extract of which he read to the House, permitted the workmen of the country, 'to combine to any extent, or in any form they pleased, with respect to the trades in which they were engaged, without subjecting themselves to any legal condemnation....' It was Wakley's opinion that, 'no Gentleman would say that the merely administering [of] the oath made them [the unions] illegal'. (Here, Wakley made a mistake with his dates: the Act 4 Geo.IV c.129 – the repeal of the Combination Acts – having been passed in the years 1824/25).

Wakley informed the House that George Loveless had, on a salary of only 7 shillings per week, 'succeeded in purchasing a small theological library, and had studied with so much assiduity that there was no man in the neighbourhood who could compete with him in point of theological knowledge.' Also, except for one individual (James Hammett) who, 'had been charged when a boy 12 years of age, with taking a piece of old iron from a farm yard, valued at fourpence,' none of them had ever been guilty of any breach of the law.

More honest, peaceable, and industrious men than these six did not exist in the whole kingdom; a fact attested to by their employers at Tolpuddle. Wakley then read out a note which he had received from a lady who had employed four of the men (George and James Loveless, and Thomas and John Standfield) for several years in the capacity of agricultural labourers.

She could confirm that, 'they were all honest and industrious men.' (This can only have been a reference to Mrs Susanna Northover of West Farm, she being the only registered female farm leaseholder in the parish at that time).

Wakley summed up his argument by stating that in his view, the Tolpuddle Society (Union), 'was legal with the single exception of the oath; and when the object was legal, the oath alone could not make the society illegal.' He, therefore, proposed, 'that an Humble Address be presented to the King praying that his Majesty would be pleased to grant a pardon to, and direct the recall of, the six Dorchester Labourers [from Australia].'

Finally, Wakley, 'entreated the noble Lord [Lord John Russell]' to take into account the large number of people who had petitioned for a remission of the sentence passed upon the men, and to take note of the, 'excitement [i.e. indignation] which the severity of their punishment had caused throughout the country.' One petition alone, for example, contained upwards of 21,000 signatures, and Wakley believed that the total number of persons who had petitioned in favour of the six men exceeded 800,000.

Despite Wakley's logical and coherent presentation of the facts to the House, and the overwhelming strength of his argument, his Motion was defeated by 308 votes to 82.[11]

1. *The True Sun*, 25 March, 1834.
2. *Hansard Parliamentary Debates*, 26 March 1834.
3. Ibid, 14 April 1834.
4. Ibid, 18 April 1834.
5. *The True Sun*, 19 and 27 April 1834.
6. *The Times*, 27 April 1834.
7. *Sherborne, Dorchester and Taunton Journal*, 1 May 1834.
8. *The True Sun*, 27 April 1834.
9. Ibid, 27 April 1834.
10. *The Pioneer*, 26 April 1834.
11. *Hansard*, op.cit., June 26, 1835.

21

A Royal Complication

It would be reassuring, to some extent, to believe that the change in attitude which came about on the part of the Establishment to the Tolpuddle Martyrs was influenced by the degree of public indignation expressed at their harsh and unreasonable treatment. However, this does now appear to have been the case, for it was through the behaviour of an entirely different group of people that it was obliged to act.

In the Summer of 1834, following the trial of the Tolpuddle Martyrs that Spring, an issue came to the fore, which, as far as the Establishment was concerned, was to muddy the waters in respect of the trial and conviction of the six men. This related to the Orange Order (Protestant Society), whose members, it transpired, had also been in the habit of swearing illegal oaths. The subject was mooted in July 1834 by the *Westminster Review*:

> It has been asked, what would be said were any of the Peers or magistrates who have taken the Orange oaths, to be sentenced to transportation. The [their] legal crime is the same as that of Loveless...[1]

A year later, on 4 August 1835, Joseph Hume M.P., announced to the House of Commons, that as far as the Orange institution of Ireland was concerned, every member was obliged to:

> ...belong to a private lodge, to which he is admitted under a religious sanction, and with a religious ceremony, carrying a bible in his hands, submitting to certain forms and declarations, and taught secret signs and passwords.

Hume then quoted the evidence given by the Reverend O'Sullivan, who described in great detail the ceremony to which he had referred.

On 12 August 1835, Thomas Wakley M.P., that staunch supporter of the Tolpuddle Martyrs, presented a petition from 5,000 inhabitants of Bristol:

...praying for a total remission of the sentence passed on the Dorchester labourers.... In presenting such a petition, he could not avoid observing upon the punishment inflicted upon those unfortunate men, and the perfect impunity with which members of Orange Lodges, who had committed as great, if not a greater offence, had been allowed to escape.

It appeared to Wakley,

...not a little extraordinary that persons of high station, of character, of great talents, and large experience, should be allowed to commit with impunity an offence such as it had been shown within the last two or three nights [of debate] the members of Orange Lodges had committed, while persons so ignorant, and so unacquainted with the law they were transgressing, as those unfortunate labourers, should be visited with the heavy punishment inflicted on them.

Wakley now explained how, prior to 1834, members of Orange Lodges (meeting places for branches of the Ulster Protestant Society) had been obliged to make:

a declaration... requiring secrecy in their proceedings, exactly similar to that taken by the Dorchester labourers.... The country would demand that these unfortunate men [the Tolpuddle Six] should not any longer be subjected to the punishment they were now undergoing after these disclosures respecting the Orange Lodges.

If all those Orangemen thus accused were not prosecuted, the people of England would be satisfied that there was one law for the rich and another for the poor in this country.[2]

Meanwhile, behind the scenes, Lord John Russell (now Home Secretary), in a letter to Lord Melbourne (now Prime Minister) dated 2 October 1835, made it clear that he, too, was far from happy with the situation:

One of the Dorchester labourers, [George] Loveless, made a confession that he had been seduced by Londoners, and had got the men [of the Tolpuddle union] to take oaths, thinking there was nothing in it against law. Upon which I wrote to the Colonial Office that the two Lovelesses should be pardoned after three years in the colony.

Russell stated, that despite his having received a letter from Joseph Hume, he did not feel disposed to take any further action in support of the six men, 'for then we should be in their power, instead of their being in ours.' He admitted, however, that the Duke of Cumberland [His Royal Highness Ernest Augustus, Prince of Great Britain and Ireland, brother of the present king, William IV, and Imperial Grand Master of the Orange Order] and the Duke of Gordon [Deputy Grand Master of the Orange Order of Scotland] were, 'far more guilty than the labourers, but the law does not reach them, I fear.'[3] This, of course, was political dynamite, because if the same legal process as had been applied in the case of the Tolpuddle Martyrs were to be applied to the Duke of Cumberland, then the latter would undoubtedly be not only found guilty of swearing an illegal oath, but also, by implication, of attempting to stir up mutiny and sedition!

Melbourne's reply to Russell of 6 October 1835 indicated that he too was:

>...certainly quite against doing anything more in the case of the Dorsetshire labourers. I thought the matter had been considered to have been settled. Perhaps if it will tend to prevent the revival of the question, you might facilitate their being joined by their families. You call Loveless's statement that he had been seduced by Londoners a confession — I call it a defence or justification, and probably false. Did he state who those Londoners were?[4]

Russell, however, told Melbourne that in his opinion the question of the Dorchester labourers was not finally disposed of. Furthermore, the debate in the House of Commons had concluded with Sir Robert Peel (M.P. for Tamworth, and formerly Prime Minister from November 1834 to April 1835) arguing that if any knowledge came to Russell which was in the Martyrs' favour, then it was quite open to him, on his responsibility, to give them a further remission. Since that time, said Russell:

>...two circumstances have transpired — one that Loveless gave a very fair, and I believe, true account, that the evidence against him was agreeable to the fact, but that he took what he did from the suggestion of others, and that he did not know it was unlawful. Now as to the unlawfulness, it required putting together two Acts of Parliament to prove that the thing was unlawful; [Daniel] O'Connell [Lawyer, M.P., and champion of Irish freedom from British rule] says now that it was lawful, and no proclamation warned them that what was notoriously

done all over London was illegal. Secondly, it appears that the Duke of Cumberland and Lord Wynford [William Draper Best, 1st Baron Wynford] have been doing the same thing only with more cunning, and deserve at least a more severe punishment. I have already offered the wives of the Lovelesses to go out [to Australia], but they would not go till their husbands were consulted. Certainly if I stay in office I shall not keep the sentence in force the whole seven years.[5]

In his reply to Russell dated 13 October 1835, Melbourne indicated that he himself had no such qualms of conscience. Quite the contrary. He now intended to wash his hands of the whole affair:

I do not myself care much what is done respecting the Dorsetshire labourers. But you know the feeling which exists against their being brought back into the Country.[6]

This latter statement was a travesty of the truth, at any rate as far as the working classes were concerned, as future events would shortly prove.

The debate about the six Tolpuddle Martys now rumbled on, largely because there were men of conscience in the House of Commons who simply would not permit the matter to rest. On 23 February 1836, Joseph Hume rekindled the debate, when he expressed to the House his opinion that the existence of Orange Lodges in the army, 'was making fearful inroads... [and] was gradually tending to sap and undermine its discipline.'

Hume estimated that there were upwards of 1,500 Lodges in Ireland, and 350 in England - the Orangemen in Ireland numbering about 200,000 men, and in England about 100,000. Not only were such Lodges a menace to the integrity of the army, but Catholics were excluded from them, it being their (the Lodges) 'avowed object' to oppose the latter's creed. The Lodges, by promoting Protestant ascendancy, and denying the majority of the people (i.e. the Catholics) their civil rights, only served to perpetuate the misery and misfortune of the Irish people. Orangemen, for example, were permitted to carry arms, whereas Catholics were not. In view of these facts, said Hume, His Majesty's Government, 'should dismiss from all civil, as well as military offices, those who were connected with the Orange institution.'

Hume reminded the House of His Majesty King William IV's orders to his commander-in-chief, 'to the effect that any military officer or soldier who attended any Orange Lodge, should be liable to be tried by a court-martial. Notwithstanding this command of His Majesty, His Royal Highness the Duke of Cumberland had, as it seemed to him, equally set at defiance the orders of the King....' The result of this was, that when the, 'lower class of Orangemen... heard that the King's brother was at the head of their society, and that he was a field marshal, they believed they could break the law with impunity.'

Hume now turned up the pressure by moving the following Resolutions. Firstly, that, 'the existence of the Orange Societies is highly detrimental to the peace of the community, by exciting discord amongst the several classes of His Majesty's subjects....' Secondly:

> ...that Orange societies, and all other political societies which have secret forms of initiation and secret signs, and are bound together by any religious ceremony, are especially deserving of the severest reprobation of the House, and should no longer be permitted to continue.

Thirdly, that:

> ...an humble Address be presented to His Majesty, that His Majesty will be graciously pleased to direct measures to be taken to remove from the public service, at home and abroad, every Judge, Privy Councillor, Lord-Lieutenant, Deputy Lord-Lieutenant, Custos Rotulorum [Keeper of the Rolls], Magistrate, Militia Officer, Inspector, Chief Constable of the Constabulary and Peace Preservation Force, every Officer of Police in Ireland, and every functionary employed in the administration of justice, and in maintaining the peace of the country, who shall attend the meeting of any Orange Lodge, of any Ribbon Lodge [Irish secret society opposed to the Orangemen], or of any other political Club, Institution, or Association, whenever, or wherever assembled, having secret forms of initiation, and being bound together by any religious ceremony, and with secret signs and passwords for recognition of Members of such bodies, and who shall not withdraw from such Societies or Associations on or before the expiration of one month after the publication of any Proclamation which His Majesty may be pleased to direct to be issued hereupon, forbidding their continuing to be Members of such Orange Lodges, Societies, and Associations.

Sir William Molesworth (Radical M.P. for East Cornwall), who rose to second the motion, took an even more strident tone; focussing his attention on the King's brother, and going so far as to brand him a criminal:

Let… the law officers of the Crown present to the Grand Jury of Middlesex bills of Indictment against the Imperial Grand Master, the Duke of Cumberland…. At his fate, none but his followers will mourn. A few years residence on the shores of the Southern Ocean [Australasia] would teach him and other titled criminals that the laws of their country are not to be violated with impunity, and that equal justice is now to be administered to the high and to the low.

Russell, in the face of such a withering onslaught, now bowed to the inevitable, and suggested the following course of action:

That an humble address be presented to His Majesty, praying that His Majesty will be graciously pleased to take such measures as his Majesty may deem advisable for the effectual discouragement of Orange Lodges, and generally of all political societies excluding [i.e which exclude] persons of different religions, and using [which use] secret signs and symbols, and acting [which act] by means of associated branches.

Mr James Sharman Crawford, Liberal M.P. for Dundalk and Rothdale, summed up the situation perfectly, saying he was:

…at a loss to understand upon what grounds the Trade Unions were declared to be illegal, even under the common law alone, in a proclamation issued some years back, unless on ground equally applicable to the Orange institutions of Ireland.[7]

Two days later, it fell to Russell to acquaint the House with the King's response to its petition:

William Rex. – I willingly assent to the prayer of the Address of my faithful Commons, that I will be pleased to take such measures as may seem to me advisable for the effectual discouragement of Orange Lodges, and generally of all political societies, excluding persons of different religious faith, using secret signs and symbols, and acting by means of associated branches. It is my firm intention to discourage all such societies in my dominions, and I rely with confidence on the fidelity of my loyal subjects to support me in this determination.[8]

The following day, 26 February 1836, Henry Maxwell (7th Baron Farnham, Irish peer) told the House that he had been directed by His Royal Highness the Duke of Cumberland, to state:

> ...that in consequence of His Majesty's wish, expressed in answer to the Address of the House of Commons, His Royal Highness [i.e. the Duke] has taken steps, in concert with all the leading members of the Orange Society now in London, to recommend to them the dissolution of that Society. And I am further directed by His Royal Highness to state that it is his intention immediately to take steps for the dissolution of the Orange Society of Great Britain and the colonies.

Russell, who had acquainted Cumberland with the above developments, now read aloud to the House the reply that he himself had received from the Duke:

> My Lord
> Before I had received your Lordship's communication I had already taken steps, in conjunction with several official and distinguished members of the Loyal Orange Institution in Ireland, to recommend its immediate dissolution, in conformity with the loyal principles of that institution. I have only to add I shall take immediate steps to dissolve the Loyal Orange Institution in Great Britain.
>
> I have the honour to be, yours sincerely,
> ERNEST.[9]

Clearly Cumberland realised, that had he not instantly capitulated, he would have risked arrest, trial, and possibly transportation. Would that the Six Men of Tolpuddle had been accorded the same opportunity that he had been given, to extricate themselves from the predicament in which they had found themselves in the Spring of 1834!

On 3 March 1836, Russell declared, that following the discussion which had taken place in the House, he now thought it his duty:

> ...to recommend to His Majesty that two of the Dorchester labourers should have a part of their sentence commuted. He had already stated that four out of the six had been [i.e. would be] permitted to return at the end of two years, which would terminate in October of the present year: and he felt it his duty to recommend to his Majesty that the remaining two [George and James Loveless] should return at the end of three years, which His Majesty had been pleased to direct.[10]

Even now, M.P. Thomas Wakley was not entirely satisfied, and on 14 March 1836 in the House of Commons, he enquired as to whether, in the light of the several petitions which he had presented, 'in favour of the mitigation of the sentence upon the two Dorchester labourers [i.e. the two Loveless brothers]', their case had been investigated.

To which Russell replied that he was able to answer Wakley's question, 'with great satisfaction. His Majesty had been pleased to grant a free pardon to the whole of the persons, who had been convicted on the occasion to which the Hon. Member referred.'[11]

On 3 April 1836, an exasperated reader wrote to the *Radical* newspaper to ask why, if the Government meant to pardon the six men, it had not done so earlier, and quoted the Latin phrase — *bis dat qui cito dat* [he gives twice, who gives promptly]. Whereupon, its Editor swiftly provided the answer:

The indictments against His Royal Illustrious Highness the Duke of Cumberland, for being at the head of an illegal society, were all but prepared and would have been sent in to the next Grand Inquest for Middlesex, had not Ministers, in a quiet way, interfered. Our readers are aware that the offence being only that of misdemeanour, though punishable by transportation, His Royal Highness would have been tried by a petty Jury. Ministers, all-bewigged as they are, were not radical enough to avoid a shudder at the thought of even the possibility of indicting a Prince of the Blood Royal, and, as to transporting his Royal Highness, only imagine a Whig so much as thinking of such a thing. As it was, however, an awkward affair, the labourers [of Tolpuddle] were pardoned to save the prince.[12]

In the light of these facts, the decision of the establishment to show clemency to the Tolpuddle Martyrs appears to be the result, not of public pressure, but of political expediency.

---

1. *Westminster Review*, July 1834, p.53.
2. *Hansard Parliamentary Debates*, 12 August 1835.
3. Russell to Melbourne, 2 October 1835, quoted in Padden, Graham (Compiler), *Tolpuddle: An Historical Account through the eyes of George Loveless*, p.45.

4. Melbourne to Russell, 6 October 1835, quoted in Padden, Graham (Compiler). *Tolpuddle: An Historical Account through the eyes of George Loveless*, p.45.
5. Citrine, Walter (Editor). *The Book of the Martyrs of Tolpuddle, 1834-1934*. London, pp.74,76.
6. *Early Correspondence of Lord John Russell* by R Russell, quoted in Padden, Graham (Compiler). *Tolpuddle: An Historical Account through the eyes of George Loveless*, p.45.
7. *Hansard*, op.cit., 23 February 1836.
8. Ibid, 25 February 1836.
9. Ibid, 26 February 1836.
10. Ibid, 3 March 1836.
11. Ibid, 14 March 1836.
12. *Radical*, 3 April 1836.

22

Transportation

From the time George Loveless and his companions were arrested on 24 February 1834, and summarily marched away to Dorchester, they and their families became victims of vindictiveness on the part of the authorities, both at home and abroad. Nevertheless, the families of the six men, despite the dire straits in which they had found themselves following the removal of their men folk, were permitted to remain in their cottages.

Loveless described how smoke from the fire in the 'miserable dungeon' at County Hall in which he had been incarcerated during the trial, had almost suffocated him, and one cannot help but form a conclusion that this was a deliberate attempt by the authorities to undermine his health, and thereby his spirit. The result was that when his five companions were escorted, on 27 March 1834, from His Majesty's Prison, Dorchester, to the *YORK* prison hulk (redundant ship) which lay anchored off Gosport in Portsmouth harbour, he, being too ill to travel, remained behind, to be treated by Dr Arden, the prison hospital's surgeon,[1] (who had the authority to order extra tea, gruel, or meat dishes to aid a prisoner's recovery.)[2] Meanwhile, Loveless's five companions were transferred from the hulk to the *SURREY*,

The YORK *hulk in Portsmouth harbour, etching by EW Cooke, 1828.*

which sailed for New South Wales (via Plymouth) on 31 March.

It was not until 5 April 1834 that George Loveless, with fetters attached to his legs, was locked onto a horse drawn coach, which took him to Salisbury, en route to the *YORK* prison hulk which his companions had left 5 days previously.[3] And when, on 25 May, he, Loveless, embarked on the convict vessel *WILLIAM METCALFE* (along with 240 other convicts), it was for a voyage, not to the mainland of Australia, to where his companions had been sent, but to Van Diemen's Land (now Tasmania).[4]   Again, the conclusion must be, that as perceived ringleader, he was singled out to be separated from his companions, and sent to what was considered to be a worse location than theirs.

Van Diemen's Land was discovered by Dutch navigator Abel Janszoon Tasman in 1642, and named by him after Anthony Van Diemen, Governor of the Dutch East India Company. It was established as a British penal colony in 1803. (Originally part of New South Wales, it became a separate colony in 1825). The threats, intimidation, and severe maltreatment suffered by the six men are described in detail by George Loveless in *The Victims of Whiggery*, and by his four companions in *The Horrors of Transportation*. (James Hammett was unable to contribute to this publication, for reasons shortly to be explained).

On 4 September 1834, the *WILLIAM METCALFE*, having sailed for 30 miles or so up the River Derwent, anchored at Hobart Town, capital of Van Diemen's Land, having journeyed approximately 14,000 miles. On 9 September, Loveless was interviewed by Mr Thomas Mason, Hobart's Assistant Police Magistrate, who questioned him closely about the union, and accused him of harbouring, 'some secret design of conspiracy' in the creation of it. If Loveless did not tell him everything, then he would report him to the Governor. Loveless would then be tried a second time, and severely punished. Mason also told his prisoner that to take an oath but not to reveal it, was a sin, 'against God and man....'[5] So what were Loveless's secrets? 'I have none to tell, Sir,' the prisoner replied.

On 12 September 1834, the men were put ashore, taken to the prisoners' barracks, and inspected by the Governor, Colonel George Arthur, who told Loveless that he had been a fool to have anything to do with trade unions. What had been his object in doing so? Loveless answered that he was attempting, 'to prevent our wives and families from being utterly degraded and starved.' "What? cannot labouring men live by their labour?" 'No, Sir, replied Loveless. There had been times in England when labour was well rewarded, but this was no longer the case. There were many 'good, willing workman' who could find no employment at all, and others who received so little for their labour, that it was 'impossible for them to live, if they have families.' "But you know that you did very wrong, do you not?" 'I had no idea whatever that I was violating any law,' replied Loveless, who failed to see, 'how a man can break a law before he knows that such a law is in existence.'[6] This was an allusion to the fact that the Tolpuddle union had been formed in late 1833, whereas the magistrates 'Caution' (which acquainted Loveless with the fact that he had broken the law), had not been displayed in Tolpuddle village until 22 February 1834.[7]

The following day, Loveless was again interrogated by Mason, who told him, that if he did not reveal his secret, he would be, 'ordered for severer punishment,' that is, forced to work, 'in irons [fetters] on the roads.' From where did this order emanate? According to the Hobart Town newspaper the *Tasmanian*, from the home government back in England.[8] Whereupon, Loveless declared that he had told Mason all he knew. Then came better news. Said Mason, 'In consequence of the conversation you had with the governor yesterday, his mind is disposed in your favour; he won't allow you to go where you was assigned to [i.e. to work on the roads]; he intends to take you to work on his farm.' This was Domain (Government) Farm, at New Town, 15 miles from Hobart.[9] Clearly, and to his credit, Governor Arthur had taken what George Loveless had told him at face value.

All through his time of tribulation, George Loveless's Christian faith did not desert him, and a measure of just how important it was to him is demonstrated by the fact that, poor as he was, he managed to summon up sufficient resources to purchase a *Holy Bible* from a fellow convict. On the *Bible*'s inner cover, Loveless wrote his name, followed by the words, 'This book bought of Joseph Walton, New Town, Van Dieman's Land.' (his spelling)[10] (Joseph Walton is on record as having been convicted of assaulting one John Hawthorne, on the New Town Road just north of Hobart, on 19 August 1829, for which he had received a fine.)[11]

At this time, the convicts in Van Diemen's Land numbered around 15,700, or about 40 per cent of the total population. Aboriginals were believed to number about 5,000. Of the convicts, 11,000, or so, were assigned to settlers, or were in possession of tickets of leave (licences to move freely about and seek work, prior to the expiration of their sentences). For those employed by the government, which included 2,600 working on chain gangs, penal settlements, or at hard labour, and 2,000 who were attached to the Public Department, the total cost of maintenance was £67,622.5s.11d per annum; the average annual cost for each convict being £14.9s.0d.[12]

Correspondence dated 20 December 1834, indicated that Governor Arthur, 'Considers this man [George Loveless] and his companions may have been the Dupes of more Artful Men' in their creation of the Tolpuddle trade union. (This was an echo of Lord John Russell, who stated on 2 October 1835, that George Loveless had told him that he [Loveless], 'had been seduced by Londoners'.)[13] However, the spirit of Christmas 1834, evidently did not percolate through to Governor Arthur's office, which on Boxing Day (26 December), requested information as to what food was necessary, 'to support a man in health when subjected to severe labour from sun rise to sun set.'[14]

During his time at Domain Farm, no fault could be found with Loveless in respect of his work, until one day, in December the following year, 1835, he was taken to the police office and charged with neglect of duty. Having listened to Loveless's reasoned arguments, the magistrate, W Gun Esq., decided that he had been assigned to more duties than he could reasonably be expected to perform, so he dismissed the case.[15] On 29 December, another magistrate, Mr Josiah Spode, enquired of Loveless whether he wished his wife and family to join him in the colony. 'Am I about to obtain my liberty?', asked Loveless. The answer was no. 'Then, Sir, I can have nothing at all to say on the subject, while I am a prisoner.' At this, the magistrate was most displeased, and threatened Loveless with "a d....d good flogging."[16]

On 7 January 1836, Mr Spode sent for Loveless, repeated his offer, and was met with the same negative reply. On 24 January, his Excellency Governor George Arthur himself visited Loveless in person and repeated the offer to bring his wife and family to him from England, 'free of expense.' This was a mark of the respect which the governor had for Loveless as a decent, honest man, and also of his regard for Loveless as a skilled and valued husbandman. However, the answer was again in the negative. 'I should be sorry to send for my wife and children to come into misery,' said Loveless. 'Why, Sir, I have seen nothing but misery since I came into this country.' He then described the conditions under which the prisoners were held as being, 'no better than slavery.' The governor then told Loveless that he was, 'a good farming man, and… a good shepherd,' and that if his wife were to join him, they could both, 'do well… in this country.' But how was he to support his wife, asked Loveless, whilst he remained a prisoner? To this, the governor answered that he would gladly grant Loveless his liberty as soon as his wife arrived, but dared not do so, it being the rule that no man sentenced to seven years transportation was to be granted, 'a ticket of leave', until he had been in the colony for a minimum of four years.[17]

Loveless promised the governor that he would consider his offer, reflecting that:

…if a man opposes the authorities, he becomes a marked man, and parties are looking out to get a case against him to entangle him. Numbers have thus fallen victims to revenge, to the utter deprivation of their reputation, property, and liberty.

Accordingly, on 27 January 1836, Loveless wrote a letter to his wife, requesting her to come to Van Diemen's Land, and sent his letter, unsealed, to the governor, acquainting him with his decision. Loveless's action quickly bore fruit. On 5 February 1837, on the orders of the governor, he was given a ticket, 'exempting him from… government labour,' and authorizing him, 'to employ himself to his own advantage, until further orders.' For Loveless, being granted this degree of liberty proved to be a mixed blessing, for he now found himself to be, 'a stranger in the colony: without money, without clothes, without friends, and without a home.' It was, therefore, with some difficulty that he found a master (employer), 'in whose service I remained until I left the country.' This was a Major de Gillern, at Glenayr near Richmond, 20 miles from Hobart.[18]

By a stroke of good fortune, de Gillern granted Loveless regular access to his newspapers, and in this way, from a copy of the *London Dispatch*, 'dated I believe, April the 2nd,' he learnt that Home Secretary Lord Russell had sent orders to Australia that, 'the Dorchester Unionists were not only to be set at liberty, but also [were] to be sent back to England, free of expense, and with every necessary comfort.' Loveless instantly made a copy of the relevant paragraph. He now allowed a period of three weeks to elapse, after which time he wrote, not to the governor, but to RL Murray, Esq., editor of the *Tasmanian*, enquiring as to whether the governor had received orders from home (England), regarding the fate of himself, and of his five colleagues on the Australian mainland.

Shortly after his letter was published in the *Tasmanian*, Loveless was summoned to Hobart Town by the governor. Meanwhile, a letter arrived from Josiah Spode of the Principal Superintendent's Office, stating that the governor intended to inform Loveless that, having been granted a free pardon, he was to be offered a free passage to England. If Loveless was willing to accept this offer, then his Excellency would give him a passage on the ship *ELPHINSTONE*.[19] Loveless's answer was as before. Whereas he, 'would most gladly embark,' nevertheless, 'it would be a dreadful thing' for his wife Elizabeth to arrive in Hobart Town, and discover that he had returned to London. Spode now became hectoring in his manner, telling Loveless that unless he availed himself of this opportunity swiftly, the government would not be able to offer him a free passage.

Eight or ten days later, Loveless travelled to Hobart Town where he met with the Colonial Secretary Lord Glenelg, and reiterated his position, pointing out in the course of the conversation that his free pardon had apparently been languishing in the office of the latter for, 'some considerable time,' before he had been informed of it. The Colonial Secretary told Loveless that this was because, 'we did not know where to send to you' [i.e. how to contact him]. "I beg your pardon, Sir, that could not be the reason, as the place I called my home was registered in the police office, by order of the Governor."

Shortly after this, Loveless was sent a copy of *Memorandum* from the Principal Superintendent's Office. It was dated 24 October 1836:

With reference to a former notification addressed to you from this office, relative to a free pardon having been ordered for you from England, I am now to inform you that his Excellency, the Lieutenant-Governor, is pleased to approve of that indulgence being issued to you immediately; and I am further to acquaint you, in consequence of your having expressed your disinclination to embark for England, by the *ELPINSTONE*, from [in consequence of his] having written some months ago to your wife, to join you with your three children in this colony, and that you are therefore anxious to await the result of that communication, that, in the event of your expectation not being fulfilled, as it regards the arrival of your family, and which an interval of three or four months may determine; his Excellency has been pleased to direct that a free passage is to be then offered you by the government that you may return to England. [Signed] Josiah Spode.[20]

Matters were at last resolved, when, on 23 December 1836, Loveless received a letter from his wife Elizabeth, informing him that she did not intend to come to Van Diemen's Land, and, 'wishing me to return as soon as possible.' The outcome was, that in the evening of Monday, 30 January 1837, Loveless set sail from Hobart Town for England aboard the ship *EVELINE*, and arrived in London on 13 June.

1. Loveless, George. *The Victims of Whiggery*, p.10.
2. The Dorchester Kelly's Directory for 1848 shows a Christopher Arden, surgeon, at High West Street, Dorchester. Source, Dorset History Centre.)
3.Dorchester Prison Records, Dorset History Centre, Microfilm R/878.
4.Loveless, George. *The Victims of Whiggery*, p.12.
5.Ibid, pp.13-14.
6. Ibid, p.14.
7. Ibid, p.14.
8. Ibid, p.18.
9. Ibid, p.15.
10. Anderson, Geoffrey R. *The Martyrs of Tolpuddle, Settlers in Canada*, p.55.
11. Archives of Tasmania.
12.Governor George Arthur, Index of Correspondence, 20 October 1835. The National Archives, Kew, CO 280/52.
13.Ibid.
14. Ibid.
15.Loveless, George, op. cit., pp.15-16.
16.Ibid, p.16.
17.Ibid, p.17.
18.Ibid, p.19.
19.Ibid, p.20.
20.Ibid, p.20.

Fate of the Other Five Men

George Loveless's four companions who were transported to the Australian mainland – rather than, as he was, to Van Diemen's Land - recounted their experiences in *The Horrors of Transportation*, published in 1838. James Hammett did not contribute to this account, as at that time, he had not yet returned from Australia.

John Standfield began by telling how, on 27 March 1834, he, his father Thomas, James Loveless, James Hammett, and James Brine were 'ironed together' and taken under escort by (horse-drawn) coach from 'Dorchester Castle' - the local name for His Majesty's Prison, so-called because it stood on Castle Hill, the site of Dorchester's former castle) to Portsmouth - where they were placed aboard the *YORK* prison hulk. Two days later, along with 100 other men, they were transferred to the ship *SURREY*, which took on another 100 men at Spithead before sailing to Plymouth, where sixty more were taken aboard. From here, they set sail on 11 April, and arrived at Sydney, capital of New South Wales, on 17 August. The abominable conditions which they encountered during that four month voyage were graphically described by John Standfield.

In 1770, British naval explorer Captain James Cook, claimed New South Wales for Britain, and in 1788 it was established as a British penal colony. Now, in 1834, it contained, approximately, 28,000 convicts (which represented over 80 per cent of the colony's population), of whom about 2,500 were females. Aboriginal numbers are not known.[1]

On 4 September 1834, the men were escorted to Sydney's Hyde Park Barracks, from where they were allocated to various masters, by whom they would be put to work. John Standfield told how he was assigned to a Mr Jones of Sydney, with whom he remained for five days. He was then sent by steam boat 100 miles (John gives the distance, erroneously, as 150 miles), to one of Jones's farms Balwarra, 3 miles from the town of Maitland on the Hunter river. After working every day from sunrise to sunset, John was obliged to sleep in a coffin-shaped, 'watch-box [small shelter, for a person on watch], 6 feet by 18 inches, with a small bed and one blanket...' which was open to the, 'starry heavens, and where the wind blew in at one end and out of the other, with nothing to ward off the peltings of the pitiless storm....' To make life even more miserable, John was obliged to travel 4 miles on foot to acquire his rations: a journey which he was, 'compelled to perform by night.'

Meanwhile, said John, his father Thomas, aged 44, was assigned to a Mr Nowlan for whom he worked as a shepherd. As Nowlan's farm was only 3 miles from Balwarra, John, after about three weeks, was permitted to visit his father, who presented to him, 'a dreadful spectacle, [being] covered with sores from head to foot, and weak and helpless as a child.' John continued to visit Thomas for nine months or so, after which time the latter was transferred to a sheep station (farm) on the Williams river. As this was 30 miles distant, John was now forbidden to visit, the overseer considering that this would be, 'too great an indulgence.'

Time passed, and on 25 January 1836, John was sent to Maitland, where he was imprisoned with neither bed nor blanket, and kept without food for two days, after which he was given only bread and water. Shortly afterwards, he was taken under guard to the court house, where his father Thomas joined him. No explanation for this maltreatment was forthcoming; the magistrates ordering that the pair be returned to the 'lock-up', where they remained under the same, miserable conditions.

Two days later, the two men, together with eight other prisoners, were chained together, taken to Morpeth on the Hunter river, and from there, sent by steamboat to Newcastle. Having been imprisoned there for three days and nights, five of the men, including the two Standfields, were sent in handcuffs – despite John Standfield's protestations - by steamboat to Sydney; a voyage of about 80 miles (John Standfield states 100). Here, they were, once again, imprisoned in the city's gaol: this time in a 'dungeon' containing 100 convicted prisoners who were awaiting the judgement from the Criminal Court. They were deprived of food, bed, blankets, or change of clothes. A week later, twenty of these 100 men were selected,   handcuffed to a long chain, and, 'marched through the streets of Sydney like a lot of wild beasts' to the Court House. Subsequently, however, the two Standfields were released from the chain and taken to Sydney's Hyde Park Barracks, where they were placed under guard.

John Standfield again protested, this time to the Barrack Superintendent Mr Foster, wishing to know why he and his father had been treated in so severe a manner. In response, all the authorities would say was that they had been taken from their masters, 'in pursuance of orders received from the home government [i.e. in England], to the effect that we were to be employed on government work only....' John interpreted this to mean that he and Thomas were to be treated, 'with the utmost severity', and he was right, because after a few days spent in the barracks, the Standfields were sent to work with a government [labouring] gang. It was while they were, 'so engaged [that] one of our Brethren, James Brine, came and joined us, and in a few days more my uncle, James Loveless, came also.

A month or so later, the four men were summoned to the Principal Superintendent's Office, and told that they were to be granted a conditional pardon by the home government, 'at the expiration of three years from our arrival in the colony.' However, an order had been received from the governor, that in the meantime, they were to proceed to the penal settlement at Port Macquarie - described as, 'a penal settlement for refractory convicts, little better than Norfolk Island' - on the mainland, 200 miles north of Sydney, where they would remain for twelve months, 'until His Majesty's [King William IV's) further pleasure should be made known.'

John Standfield, having no wish to go to Port Macquarie, petitioned the governor on 10 March 1836, that he, his father James Loveless, and James Brine (James Hammett had not then appeared), be returned to their former masters instead. His request was granted, and the Standfields were duly sent to a sheep station belonging to their former master Mr Nowlan, situated on the Williams river and about 30 miles from Maitland. During this period, Thomas Standfield fell severely ill and was confined to his bed for a period of two months.

Nine months later, John Standfield was told by a friend that his uncle George Loveless, was in Van Diemen's Land. He immediately wrote him a letter, dated 27 November 1836, and the following February, received a reply, 'informing us that he was going to sail for England, and giving us directions in what manner we could obtain a passage for ourselves.' John immediately wrote to his other uncle, George's brother James, acquainting him with the good news, and, 'requesting him to make application for our passage... Great delay took place in consequence of Mr [John] Brennen, the Principal Superintendent, wishing to keep us in the colony; but by my uncle's perseverance a passage was at last obtained.' In all that time, said John, 'not the slightest communication was ever made to me or my companions by any government officer of our free pardon having been received.'

James Loveless, brother of George, told how he was assigned to a master at Strathallan (now Goulburn), 100 miles south west of Sydney (stated by James to be 300 miles): a journey that he made on foot, and which took 14 days. Here, he worked for the next 19 months, until in February 1836, he was returned to the barracks in Sydney where he remained for three months, not knowing what his fate was to be. Finally, he was summoned to the office of Superintendent Brennen, who told him that if he agreed to having his wife and family brought out to him from England, then the governor would grant him a free pardon as soon as they arrived. James considered the offer, then declined it, telling Brennen, that, when he obtained his liberty, it was his intention to return to England. When Brennen voiced the opinion that James, 'could do better here than at home,' the latter's reply mirrored that which his brother George had made when faced with similar circumstances: 'I think not, sir. I have seen nothing but misery in the colony.'

James Brine was assigned, first to Dr Mitchell, surgeon of the government hospital, and soon afterwards to the farm of Robert Scott, Esq. at Glindon on the Hunter river, to which he made the first part of the journey by steam-boat. However, having disembarked and lain down under a gum-tree to get some rest, he was robbed during the night by bush rangers (outlaws) who stole his small bed, his blanket, a, 'suit of new slops [garments], and one shilling;' all provided for him by his new master. Finally, on 7 September 1834, and after a 30 mile trek on foot, he arrived, exhausted, at the farm at Glindon, having consumed only one meal in the previous three days. His overseer now took him to his master who refused to believe his story about the bush rangers, and threatened him with a flogging.

The following morning, Brine was put to work digging post-holes, despite being in a weakened condition, and suffering with feet, which after his long journey undertaken without shoes, 'were so cut and sore I could not put them to the spade.' Brine was only able to overcome this difficulty by wrapping a piece of iron hoop, which he had found, around his foot for protection. For the next six months, until he 'became due' (i.e. was permitted to receive his allowances of food, clothing, etc.) he, 'went without shoes, clothes, or bedding, and lay on the bare ground at night.' Matters worsened even further when he was allocated the task of sheep washing, which involved working for seventeen days, chest high, in water. As a result, he caught a severe cold, but when he asked his master for something with which to cover himself at night - even a piece of horse-cloth would have sufficed - his request was refused.

Brine's master told him that, as he understood it, it was his [Brine's]:

>...intention to have murdered, burnt, and destroyed every thing before you, and you are sent over here to be severely punished, and no mercy shall be shown you. If you ask me for any thing before the six months is expired, I will flog you as often as I like.

Towards the end of the year 1835, Brine was sent, first to Maitland, where he was imprisoned for two days and nights with only 12 ounces of bread and half a pint of cold water in each period of twenty-four hours to sustain him. On the third day, he was chained to fifteen other prisoners, and put aboard a steam-boat bound for Newcastle, 15 or so miles away. Here, he was again imprisoned, for a fortnight. Finally, he was chained to twenty or so other men, and once again put aboard a steam boat, bound now for Norfolk Island:

>...the worst and most terrible of all the penal settlements, where those only of the convicts who have committed some heinous offence are sent, and where punishments the most inhuman and cruel are daily practiced by the authorities upon the unfortunate and wretched prisoners.

Fate intervened in the form of a gale which blew the ship back to Newcastle. After another three days of imprisonment, Brine was taken to Sydney, and again, locked in the cells; this time with men who had been condemned (presumably to death). When Brine protested, and asked to know what charge was lodged against him, he was transferred to the barracks. He protested again, and was now treated more humanely by being transferred to the 'wards' (separate rooms) and provided with a blanket. The following morning, Brine saw a sight which must have gladdened his heart: 'I saw, to my great satisfaction, two of my brethren in captivity, Thomas and John Standfield; and, in a few days after, James Loveless.'

James Loveless and James Brine, like the Standfield's, were threatened by Brennen with being sent to Port Macquarie, but in the event Brennen offered them both work on his own farm at Prospect, 22 miles from Sydney. According to James, on 17 August 1836, an advertisement appeared in *The Sydney Gazette*, stating that, 'James Hammett, James Brine, and Thomas and John Standfield, were to have a conditional pardon after having been two years in the colony, and James Loveless after being three years in the colony.' Brennen told James that the reason for him being required to serve an

136

additional twelve months longer than his companions, was that the home government considered him to be one of the ring-leaders of his, 'secret combination' (union). In fact, said Brennen, James was fortunate not to have been hanged for high treason! James was then sent to another of Brennen's farms at Kurrajong (which he spelt 'Kurryjung'), 30 or so miles from Sydney. Here, he remained until December 1836, when a friend told him that he had seen a newspaper report stating that he had been granted a free pardon. James immediately set out for Sydney, where the Superintendent of Convicts confirmed that he was now a free man, and that had it not been for a mistake by his secretary, he would have obtained his pardon sooner.

Finally, on 11 September 1837, the four men set sail from Sydney, aboard the ship *JOHN BARRY*, arriving in Plymouth on Saturday 17 March 1838, having called at New Zealand to collect some timber.[2]

✤ ✤ ✤

What of James Hammett, who was unable to contribute to *The Horrors of Transportation*, since, at the time of its publication, he was still in Australia? In fact, little is known about his time there, although a brief account was published some four decades later, in 1875, in *The Dorset County Express*.

Hammett was assigned to farmer Edward Eyre at Woodlands near Queanbeyan, 150 miles south west of Sydney; a journey which he was obliged to make on foot. According to Mrs Mary Hammett, his niece, James pleased his employer by digging a well, which was known as 'Hammett's Well'.[3]

In May 1836, Hammett reappears at Sydney's Hyde Park Barracks, sent there on the orders of the Governor of New South Wales, Sir Richard Bourke. (According to Mary Hammett, James, 'had first learned of his pardon from a newspaper left by his employer on one of his visits to Hammett's [sheep] station.')[4] However, by this time, his four companions, who had been 'rounded up' in a similar way, had already departed from there.

The next news of Hammett occurs on 20 February 1839, when he presents a 'memorial' (written statement) to the newly appointed Governor of New South Wales, Sir George Gipps, pointing out, that although he had been granted a free pardon in 1836, he had, in September of that year, been, 'unfortunately detained at Windsor [25 miles from Sydney] charged with assault....' He was now, 'anxious to return to his native land.'[5] The outcome

137

was that Hammett's passage to England was speedily authorised and, 'charged to the funds applicable to the Convict Services.'[6] Hammett duly sailed from New South Wales (presumably from Sydney) to England on 8 March 1839, on the ship *EWERETTA*. This was 2 years and 2 months after George Loveless had sailed from Van Diemen's Land, and 1 year and 6 months after his other four companions had sailed from New South Wales.

As already mentioned, the most curious fact of all in relation to James Hammett is one that is greatly to his credit, for his was a case of mistaken identity (a fact which he himself acknowledged in 1875). 'I belonged to the Union, but I was not there in the lodge at the time the men swore I was. It was my brother John...'[7] In other words, James had not been present at the Standfield's cottage when the illegal oath was sworn, but he had selflessly concealed this fact and suffered the penalty in order to protect his younger brother.

1.State Records Authority, Kingswood, New South Wales.
2.The Tolpuddle Martyrs, *The Horrors of Transportation*, pp.7-12, and pp.13-14.
3.Warwick University Modern Record Centre, *Memorandum of Interview*, dated 27 January 1934, Present, Mrs Hammett and Mr Wray, Mss. JW/EG/612.
4.Ibid.
5. Archives Authority of Sydney, New South Wales, C.S.I.L. 39/2147.
6. Ibid, C.S.I.L. 39/2497.
7. *Dorset County Express*, 23 March 1875.

24

The Return of the 'Martyrs'

When George Loveless returned to England on 13 June 1837 aboard the ship *EVELINE*, he was welcomed by the London Central Dorchester Committee, none of whose members would have been more pleased to see him than his younger brother Robert. Otherwise, George's arrival in London drew little comment from the press, which was preoccupied at that time with the failing health of the King, William IV, who died one week later on June 20.

George Loveless's father Thomas, was now aged 75, and the joy and relief which he must have felt at the safe return of his son can hardly be imagined. Sadly, Thomas did not live to see the safe return of his other son James, along with Thomas and John Standfield and James Brine, nine months later, for he died in January 1838. He was buried in the grounds of Tolpuddle's parish church on the last day of that month. John Standfield himself describes the homecoming:

After a rough and boisterous voyage we arrived in Plymouth Sound on Saturday March 17, 1838, and landed in that town on the same day, having been absent just four years. We were very kindly received by Mr. Morgan, [landlord] of the Dolphin Inn, Barbican Quay, and as soon as it was known in the town who we were, many of the inhabitants came to visit us. On the 18th Mr. James Keast, of the Friendly Society of Operative Bricklayers, very kindly invited us to his house, where we remained during our stay in the town. Several members of the above society waited upon us, and expressed a wish that we should remain a few days in the town, as they intended calling a public meeting of the working men to congratulate us on our return. Though anxious to see our families, we could not but comply with their request, after having received so much kindness from them, and on the following day a public meeting was advertised to be held at the Mechanics Institute [Princes Square, Plymouth]. The meeting was very numerously attended, and we received their hearty congratulations on our return. The next day we left Plymouth and proceeded through Exeter, where we were also welcomed by a public meeting, to our native village, Tolpuddle, Dorsetshire, arriving in safety to the great joy of our relatives and friends. [In fact, the party stopped briefly at Dorchester to change horses, and accept refreshment offered by the landlord of the Antelope Inn.][1]

A few days later, the four men, together with George Loveless with whom they had been reunited, were taken to London, where the London Central Dorchester Committee had organised a procession in their honour. This took place on 16 April, Easter Monday, and was followed by a dinner at White Conduit House, attended by some 2,000 people, including, according to *The Morning Chronicle*, 'a vast multitude of mechanics and labourers....' After dinner, The Reverend Dr Arthur S Wade, D.D., Vicar of St Nicholas, Warwick, 'having acknowledged the gift of the food in the normal way... thanked Almighty God for the return of the Dorchester labourers from beyond the seas....'

He begged of God now to bless the Dorchester labourers in restoring them to the circle of their family and that he might dispose the hearts of all true servants and all sincere Christians and good men now liberally to assist these men, that their brethren might be enabled each to 'sit under his own vine and his own fig-tree, and that no man should make them afraid.'...

Thomas Wakley, M.P., who had campaigned so eloquently and so ardently for the men in the House of Commons, 'then advanced, amidst reverberating cheers, to propose the first toast....' He suggested that:

...the labourers should be labourers no longer. Let them [the assembled company] make farmers of them all. Trifling contributions throughout the country would make them quite independent; there was a good sum of money in hand already... and they would soon have the rest.[2]

(James Hammett was, of course, included in Wakley's plans, even though he had not, as yet, returned from Australia).

On 19 April 1838, the *Plymouth and Devonport Weekly Journal* reported:

Monday being the day appointed for the celebration of the liberation and return of the Dorchester labourers by a public procession through the metropolis and a dinner at White Conduit House [London], various members of the different working classes began to assemble as previously arranged on Kennington Common as early as 7 o'clock, but up to half past eight the numbers were very small. Before nine, however, several thousands of operatives all attired in their holiday clothing had arrived on the common. Several of the trades arrived on the ground in procession, preceded by their colours and bands of music. Amongst those most distinguished for the gaiety of their display were the farriers, the whitesmiths [workers in tinned or white iron], the bricklayers and blacksmiths, the tinplate workers and glassblowers.

About a quarter before ten, a general huzza [hurrah] announced the arrival of the Dorchester labourers. They were in an open carriage drawn by four fine grey horses, and, as they were drawn through the lines, acknowledged the congratulations of the assembled thousands of their brother labourers by remaining uncovered and repeatedly bowing to all within view.

About quarter past ten, two rockets were discharged as a signal that all was ready for departure; after a short delay the procession began to move forwards towards their destination. There was not a policeman to be seen on the common, and the presence of any was certainly not required, for good order, decorum, and respectability of deportment characterised all present. Indeed the manner in which everything was conducted was highly creditable to all the parties concerned...[3]

In May 1838, the London Central Dorchester Committee responded to Wakley's suggestion, by launching the Dorset Labourers' Farm Tribute; the money raised by it to be used for the purpose of purchasing two farms in Essex, together with farm equipment for the Tolpuddle men. By August 1838, George and James Loveless, and James Brine were installed at the 80 acre New House Farm, Greenstead, and the Standfields at Fenners Farm, High Laver, about 5 miles away. According to *The Morning Post*, however, it soon became clear that farming would not be the sole preoccupation of the labourers:

The new settlers... had not been long established among the hitherto quiet and well-conducted population of these parishes before they began to agitate, and to agitate in a manner and with a degree of success which showed but too plainly that their mission of mischief had not been entrusted to unpractised or unskilful hands. Chartist [supporters of democratic political reform] newspapers were quickly seen in active circulation. The beer-shops in which they were to be found became more frequented and more noisy than heretofore. A Chartist Association was formed at Grinstead, and, by the combined or alternate influence of persuasion and of terror, nearly the whole of the agricultural labourers in that and adjoining parishes were induced to join it. A weekly subscription was exacted from each of them, and they were told that when their fund amounted to a certain sum it would be increased by the committee in London. Frequent meetings were held — the time selected for this purpose being generally on Sunday morning, during the hours of divine service. The meetings became progressively more and more numerous. At first the farmhouse occupied by the new settlers was large enough to contain them, but ere long the farmyard was found insufficient, and the assemblies were held in an adjoining field. Delegates attended the meetings from Waltham Abbey, Epping, Harlow, Broadoak, Hatfield, &c. &c. Delegates and orators from London, sometimes to the number of forty, were also occasionally present. The project of a general rising of the Chartists on or about the 12th of August was discussed and entertained. The effect of these proceedings was to diffuse a general sense of insecurity throughout that part of the country, and so far to disturb the habitual relation between the farmers and labourers...

Meanwhile, on a personal note, on 20 June 1839, James Brine married Thomas and Dianne Standfield's daughter Elizabeth. In the same year, George and Elizabeth Loveless's daughter Louisa was born.

When James Hammett, the last of the six men to leave Australasia, finally returned to England in late December 1838/early January 1839 (precise date unknown), his wife Harriett, travelled to London to greet him. Hammett's arrival did not go unnoticed by the London Central Dorchester Committee, who saw this as a further opportunity for fund raising. That September, *Cleave's Penny Gazette of Variety and Amusement* carried the following advertisement, impressing on the public that money was still required in order that the payments on the farm leases should be completed:

THE LONDON DORCHESTER COMMITTEE respectfully announce to their friends, the Members of Trade Societies, and the Public generally, that they have engaged the above commodious theatre [London's Victoria theatre, subsequently known as the 'Old Vic'] for a FAREWELL BENEFIT, on TUESDAY, OCTOBER 8th, in aid of the Dorchester Labourers Fund; when will be presented an HISTORICAL PLAY, a FAVOURITE FARCE, and a variety of other entertainment. In the course of the evening, the Dorchester labourers, with J Hammett, the last man returned, will return thanks for the public support afforded them...

The committee, in thus making a final appeal to the public, earnestly impress upon their friends the fact that unless they are enabled to raise immediately about the sum of one hundred pounds, there is a probability of a considerable portion of the monies previously subscribed being rendered comparatively useless.

The committee, upon the faith of a resolution passed at a public meeting at the Crown and Anchor in May 1838, invested the fund then in hand in the purchase of small farms whereon to place the men, the sum required to make up the purchase money (between four and five hundred pounds) being guaranteed by a general penny subscription. But 162 pounds of the sum was raised, and the men, though with every prospect of doing well by labour and perseverance, are at a complete standstill until the above sum of one hundred pounds is made up. Under these circumstances... the committee trust their friends will rally round and support them as on former occasions.[4]

The newspaper proceeded to describe the event itself:

The long-announced farewell benefit of the Dorchester labourers took place at the Victoria Theatre on Tuesday the 8th inst., on which occasion the house was literally crowded to suffocation... At the conclusion of the second piece, the curtain ascended, and discovered the great attraction of the night — the Dorchester labourers - accompanied by Mr [G] Tomey [blacksmith and member of the London Central Dorchester Committee], who stood in a row in the centre of the stage, and were greeted with one of the most enthusiastic bursts of approbation ever heard within these walls... The majority of the audience rose, whilst the pittites [those who frequented the pit of the theatre] hurled gilded wreaths of evergreen (one for each labourer) upon the stage. As soon as the tumult had subsided, Mr

143

Tomey advanced and said, 'Ladies and Gentlemen, I appear on the part of the committee, to present to you four of the six Dorchester labourers.'

Tomey then declared that he had just received a letter, informing him that the remaining two men, James Loveless and Thomas Standfield, were unable to be present, as they were attending to matters relating to their farm in Essex. He then introduced George Loveless, described as, 'a thin, pale-looking individual, who has evidently not yet recovered from the base and brutal treatment to which the Whigs subjected him....' However, as Loveless stepped forward:

> ...his agitation was so great that he was quite overcome, and his voice all but left him. The warmth of his reception aroused him a little, however, and after a moment's pause he proceeded to thank the public for the support afforded to him and his wife and family, both during and since his unjust transportation.

> The situation of this generous-souled man was heart-stirring, and excited the sympathy of all. Would to God his base persecutors had been present - they must have been moved at witnessing such a scene. Poor Loveless, eventually overcome, retired back to his companions and gave vent to his feelings in a flood of tears.

It was now John Standfield's turn:

> ...to thank his audience for the support he had received ever since he fell under, 'the claws of his oppressors', at which there was a perfect hurricane of applause. He was determined, he said, to bear all the attacks of tyranny with as great fortitude as he had done his unjust transportation (applause). He thanked the Dorchester Committee for their unceasing exertions, and the public for their generosity, and expressed the conviction that whenever any great object was to be attained, they needed nothing but union, a determined union, to achieve it (tremendous applause).

Standfield, however, was cut short by the management, much to the disgust of the editor of *The Penny Gazette*, who observed that the current 'liberal government' had, 'so far succeeded in terrifying all who... depend upon a licence... whether [for] a theatre or a public house.' For it was the government's view that the words 'Chartism' and 'sedition' were to be regarded as synonymous.[5] In December 1839, *The Morning Post* took the opposite line, agreeing with the government and describing the Chartist organisation as, 'this foul infection', which had, 'pervaded even the quiet and secluded hamlets of the county of Essex.'[6]

Initially, James Hammett joined the Lovelesses and the Brines in Essex. However, James's wife Harriett made it clear that she wished to return to Tolpuddle, and this is why Hammett returned to his home village.[7]

In that month of December 1839, there was more to celebrate, when James and Elizabeth Brine had their first child, a daughter Mary. In 1840, George and Elizabeth Loveless followed suit with another daughter Sina, and Martyr John Standfield married Elizabeth Thurgood. In 1841, the Brines had a second daughter, Susannah, and the Standfields had their first child Julian. In 1843, the Standfields had their second child Theophilus. In 1844, the Brines had their third daughter Charity. In 1845, the Standfields had their third child, also Charity.

1.The Tolpuddle Martyrs. *The Horrors of Transportation*, p.12.
2. *The Morning Chronicle*, 17 April 1838.
3. *Plymouth and Devonport Weekly Journal*, 19 April 1838.
4.*Cleave's Penny Gazette of Variety and Amusement*, 28 September 1839.
5. Ibid, 19 October 1839.
6. *The Morning Post*, 17 December 1839.
7.Warwick University Modern Record Centre, *Memorandum of Interview*, dated 27 January 1934, Present, Mrs Hammett and Mr Wray, Mss. JW/EG/612.

25

A Wronged Man Responds

There were many reasons why George Loveless was not enamoured of the Anglican Church. One was because of the way it had kept silent over the disgraceful scenes which had occurred at the opening of Tolpuddle's Wesleyan Chapel, back in 1818, when an unruly mob had attacked the Methodist ministers and their party, who had come from Weymouth to attend the ceremony. Where was the village constable on that occasion? Nowhere to be found. And why? No doubt, because he had received orders from the local magistrates to turn a blind eye to the event. And as for The Anglican Church, its hierarchy no doubt relished the discomfiture of those who, in its eyes, practised a Dissenting religion. Another reason was the behaviour of the Anglican Vicar of Tolpuddle, The Reverend Thomas Warren, who had betrayed Loveless and his companions over the matter of their weekly wages in 1831/32.

A letter sent to London's *The Morning Chronicle* and published in its columns on 2 April 1834, reveals the personal suffering which George Loveless himself was obliged to endure on account of his beliefs. The sender signed himself 'a Wesleyan':

> Several of these poor men have been known to the writer for many years, and though now far distant from them, yet in their distress he is distressed. In reference to those he knows, and especially George Loveless, that for inoffensive conduct, for diligence, for efforts to support themselves and families, and indeed for general good moral character, they will not suffer in comparison with any labourers in any county.

> Sir, they were truly guilty of one crime... In this Protestant country they committed the great crime of reading their Bible – of daring to think for themselves on what they read – of doing more, they became Members of The Wesleyan Methodist Society.... But the climax – the head and front of their offending was this – George Loveless and one

146

or two more became steady and useful preachers among the local Wesleyan Methodists. On this account, the Lovelesses and others whom I could mention in the villages of Tolpuddle, Dewlish and Piddletown, have long been the subject of bitter and unrelating persecutions.

The writer then gives the names of several eminent people in the locality, more than one of whom could testify to:

...the violence of mobs; of the refusal of a clergyman to take his dead babe into the church because it had been baptized by a Wesleyan minister, while there was no archdeacon to be found to be mediator; of a forgery to keep this very George Loveless from preaching in one of the villages; of direct attempts to starve him out of the village. [The nature of this forgery is not known].

The writer concludes by saying, 'When mighty men contend with peasants, the latter has need of great care.'

The editor of *The Morning Chronicle* was clearly of the same opinion:

That Loveless, in particular has been the object of persecution in Dorchester, because he is a local preacher, we can well believe; because the Wesleyan Methodists, being in earnest about religion, have from the outset, been encountered [i.e. suffered] by persecution from the Church in every direction. John Wesley's *Journal*, is a record of persecution instigated by Clergy of the Church of England against Methodists, during the whole of his long career which terminated in 1790. Dr Randolph, the Bishop of London... pointed out the Wesleyans in his charges as [being] particularly obnoxious, on account of their daring to assume relationship with the Church, which made them so much more dangerous than open enemies.[1]

As if this, and his transportation to Van Diemen's Land, were not sufficient punishment, George Loveless now found himself under attack from another gentleman of the cloth: this time The Reverend Henry Walter, Vicar of Hazelbury Bryan in North Dorsetshire (spelt Haselbury by Loveless), and this gave the former an opportunity to redress the balance.

In a letter to The Reverend Walter, sent from Tolpuddle in February 1838, Loveless began with a quotation from the poet John Milton: 'Give me the liberty to think, to speak, and to argue freely according to conscience, above all other liberties.' He proceeded to give vent to all the feelings of the hurt, frustration, and, above all, indignation which had long been brewing in his breast, and most acutely since his trial, sentence, and transportation, along with his five colleagues. This was his golden opportunity to hammer home, point by point, all his grievances against the established church, which he did, in his characteristically articulate and eloquent way. In fact, his letter was given wide publicity, when in the same year, its text was published, in full, by the London Dorchester Committee:

REVEREND SIR, — In addressing myself to you I adopt the above as my motto, believing that liberty of conscience is every man's birthright; and as the Almighty Creator of man hath blest me in common with others with thinking and reasoning powers, I consider that I should be abusing those noble powers, were I to be silent at the present time and not to speak out boldly and freely in vindication of truth and justice; that I should be withholding an important obligation I owe to my fellow men; and that in so doing I should reproach my Maker and sin against my own soul.

My reason, sir, for thus addressing you is the liberty taken lately with my name by several gentlemen of the clerical order, but especially by yourself. Had you confined your observations to the circle of your own friends, or even to your own parish, I should not have thought it worth my trouble to have noticed it; but as you chose to address others besides your own religious body — to represent, or rather to misrepresent, my character and conduct to them — I have thought it my duty to reply to those calumnies.

Loveless went on to question why Walter had felt it necessary to write to the President of the Wesleyan Conference, 'concerning one of whom the president most likely knows nothing and perhaps cares as little [i.e. Loveless himself]?' Had he done this in order, 'to weaken the influence and to bring into contempt an humble and obscure individual?' Loveless now quoted English poet Edward Young's poem 'Night Thoughts on Life, Death and Immortality': 'Mighty ocean into tempest wrought? To waft a feather or to drown a fly?'

Since his return to England from Australia, said Loveless, he had set before the public, 'a brief but plain statement of facts in reference to my trial and banishment....' This, however, appeared to be by no means to the liking, 'of a certain "order" of gentlemen,' and it came as no surprise to Loveless to hear one such gentleman (i.e. Walter) accuse him of, 'writing palpable falsehoods.' To this, he could only reply that, 'those that have known me longest will know best if I am capable of falsifying or not...', or, for that matter, capable of being 'a strife-maker' and 'a peace-breaker'.

Loveless was aware that his recent visit to Walter's village, and his address to those of Walter's parishioners who chose to hear him, had greatly displeased the vicar, and yet Loveless had done nothing to impugn either the public, or private character of Walter, either as a minister, or as a Christian. By what right, therefore, did Walter, 'thus stigmatise and cast reproach' upon his conduct?

Loveless now broadened his line of attack, taking the battle to what he perceived as the principal enemy, the Church of England. Its character, he says:

> ...appears of the blackest description; we behold things which make our hearts throb with indignation. After the Reformation [of the 1530s, whereby the English Church rejected the authority of the Roman Catholic Church], the inquisition [tribunal for prosecuting heresy] was as completely set up in England as in the old priest-ridden countries; and how its powers were exercised may be seen in too fearful colours on the broad page of English history, and also in the more full relations of the nonconformists and dissenters. Clergymen who could not mould their consciences at the will of the state, were ejected without mercy from their livings, and with their families exposed to all the horrors of poverty, contempt, and persecution. What a picture have we set before us of the dreadful persecutions and privations experienced by the Society of Friends [Quakers], inflicted [on them] by the clergy, and the magistrates incited by them; fines, imprisonment and death, confiscations of goods, destruction of their places of worship, age not spared, and their women treated with brutal indecency; clergymen declaring they 'would rather see all the Quakers hanged than lose a sixpence by them!'

In Loveless's view, a major stumbling block was that this same spirit of

149

repression persisted in the minds of the clergy, even in the present day. The Church of England, he said, 'considers that it has a monopoly, where religion is concerned.' He had even heard a preacher tell his parishioners that their prayers 'would be of no avail whatever unless offered up in the Established Church!' On another occasion, he had heard a minister of the church preach a sermon to the effect that, 'The true and only true church of Christ is the Church of England as established by law…,' and that, 'Roman Catholics and the different bodies of Dissenters [such as Methodists] were joining with infidels to trample on the Bible and trying to overturn the church.'

It was Loveless's opinion that those who described themselves as Christians would do well to imitate the conduct of the so-called 'infidels', by, 'entering the abodes of wretchedness and want; sympathising with the weak and afflicted; assisting the stranger, the fatherless, and the widow,' instead of standing aloof, passing by, or treating with indifference, and sometimes even with contempt, 'the objects of misery that surround them.' Of the two, whose conduct came nearest to the precepts laid down in the gospel of Christ? And he quotes from the *Holy Bible*, St Matthew, Chapter 25, verses 35, 36, and 40:

I was hungry and ye fed me, naked and ye clothed me, sick and in prison, and ye visited me; forasmuch as ye did it to the least of these my brethren ye did it unto me.

Loveless agreed with the commonly held belief that the church was in danger on account of its too close relationship with the State, and the bigotry and intolerance of its members. For instance, he knew of landed gentry who refused, absolutely, either to let land, or to employ a person, unless that person first undertook not to give encouragement to Dissenters, nor to worship in any place other than the established church. Likewise, he knew of clergymen who treated Dissenters in the same way as the Jews of Biblical times treated the Samaritans, and would have no dealings with them.

As for the assumption that, 'if we had no state religion, we should soon have no religion at all,' Loveless questioned whether religion required 'grandeur', 'pomp of state', 'the smiles of the great, the wisdom of the learned, or the wealth of the mighty' in order for it to flourish. After all, had not the Redeemer told his disciples to, 'provide neither gold nor silver, nor brass in your purses; neither scrip [paper money] for your journey; neither two coats, neither two shoes,' but instead instructed them to, 'go into all the world and preach the Gospel,' with the promise that, 'lo I am with you always until the end of the world.'

Loveless also took issue with the church over its view that an unbaptised child may not be regarded as a human being, 'until their [the clergy's] mummery has ennobled it [i.e. by baptism].' The sooner the, 'webs of the clerical spider' were removed, 'not only from the limbs but from the souls of men,' the better, said Loveless.

He berated the clergy for supporting the 'impressing' (forcible drafting) of poor people into the armed services; making a mockery of the words of the Prayer Book of 1662, (which in turn echoes the 6th Commandment of God): 'Thou shalt do no murder,'[2] and also of the words of St Matthew, 'blessed are the peace-makers.'[3]

The clergy, said Loveless, 'are ever foremost in opposing any popular measure that is likely to be carried for the good of the people,' and he cited its opposition to the Reform Bill (which extended the franchise to working people), and its support for, 'that most cruel, unchristian, arid inhuman law,' the Poor Law Amendment Act (which restricted the access of the poor to assistance ('poor relief'). What chance, he asked, did a labouring man have of obtaining justice, if his local clergyman was, 'ill-disposed towards him,' and, on this account, blocked his appeal to the magistrate for relief, simply by failing to provide the necessary written note, the production of which was obligatory if his case was to be heard?

Loveless did not refrain from pointing out, however, that, 'The undue influence... of the clergy over various degrees and orders of society' was, 'greatly on the decline.' The poor could no longer be kept in the dark and hoodwinked. Despite having been, 'kept in poverty and degradation' by those who lived in, 'luxury and idleness upon the fruits of their [the workers'] labour,' and were told that their 'portion' was, 'to labour, to suffer, and to die,' they were now convinced of their, 'unalienable right to receive a sufficient maintenance from the land that gave them birth.'

Loveless now expounded his own credo. The, 'first great object[ive]' of the labouring classes, he said, must be to achieve their, 'emancipation from mental and political slavery.' It was his belief:

...that the earth was given to man for an inheritance and not to become the property of individuals; that if any man will not work he

151

ought not to eat; that all property honestly acquired should be held sacred and inviolable; that all governments and laws should exist for the common benefit, protection, and security of all the people, and not for the emolument or aggrandizement of any particular family, single man, or set of men.

And how were these aims to be achieved? By the, 'increased spread of knowledge,' which would soon, 'scatter its healing, saving, and benign influence over and around the darkness and ignorance of the human mind....' Finally, having learnt that union is strength, and knowledge is power, the poor labourers would unite, 'in all their moral dignity... shake off the trammels of despotism,' and demand their just rights.

Loveless's letter to The Reverend Walter concluded by him expressing his belief that once the, 'appendages and mystifications of priestcraft' were stripped away, the principles of morality, justice, love, and charity, as enunciated in The Bible, would prevail and endure.[4]

1. The Morning Chronicle, 2 April 1834.
2. *Holy Bible*, Exodus, Chapter 20, Verse 13.
3. Ibid, St Matthew, Chapter 5, Verse 9.
4. Loveless, George. *The Church Shown Up*, pp.2-16.

26

Canada

E xactly when, and for what reason, five of the men of Tolpuddle decided to emigrate is not known. Perhaps they had wearied of the struggle to make their voices heard. And yet their sense of belief in their cause - which was the emancipation of working people – was by no means undimmed. They now longed to make a fresh start. So why Canada? Possibly, because they were in communication with a fellow Methodist minister there. This will be discussed shortly.

The first Europeans to arrive in Canada had found the land occupied by native Algonquin and Iroquois, who existed by hunting and fishing. From 1689, there were a series of conflicts between British and French would-be colonists, which culminated in 1763, with the Treaty of Paris, by which France ceded Canada to Britain. In 1791, the country was divided into Upper Canada (much of modern day Ontario), and Lower Canada (much of modern day Quebec). Each colony had its own legislative assembly, administered by a lieutenant-governor. 1812-1814 saw attempted invasions of both provinces by the USA; these were repelled. In 1841, Upper and Lower Canada were united as the Province of Canada (which was granted self government in 1848.)

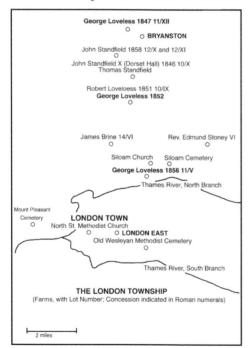

George Loveless 1847 11/XII
○
○ BRYANSTON
John Standfield 1858 12/X and 12/XI
○
John Standfield X (Dorset Hall) 1846 10/X
Thomas Standfield
○
Robert Loveloess 1851 10/IX
George Loveless 1852
○

James Brine 14/VI   Rev. Edmund Stoney VI
○   ○
Siloam Church   Siloam Cemetery
○   ○
George Loveless 1856 11/V
○
Thames River, North Branch

Mount Pleasant
Cemetery   LONDON TOWN
○   North St. Methodist Church
○   ○ LONDON EAST
Old Wesleyan Methodist Cemetery
○

Thames River, South Branch

THE LONDON TOWNSHIP
(Farms, with Lot Number; Concession indicated in Roman numerals)

2 miles

Plan of the London Township
(after Geoffrey R Anderson)

James Brine. Photo: Karen Munro Caple.

*John Standfield with his wife Elizabeth.
Photo: Gary Standfield.*

George and James Loveless and James Brine and their families, were the first to reach Canada in the Spring of 1844,[1] their destination being the London Township, situated in south-eastern Ontario, with Lake Huron to the north-west, Lake Erie and the USA to the south, and Lake Ontario to the east. London, first settled in 1826, had been so-named, by its Governor, John Graves Simcoe, after the capital of England. In the same way, the local river was renamed The Thames. Subsequently, a British garrison was stationed here. In 1832, the region was ravaged by a cholera epidemic. According to an article in *Farmers Sun*, George and his wife Elizabeth, on their arrival, were offered accommodation by Edmund Stoney (Stoney is spelt 'Storey' in the article in *Farmers Sun*), the London Township's first Methodist minister, who had been ordained in 1826.

Two years later, in 1846, the Lovelesses and the Brines were joined by Martyr Thomas Standfield and his family, including his son, Martyr John. Having started a new life in Canada, the men had an understanding with each other not to reveal their past, and it was not until after their deaths that their descendents became fully aware of their eventful and traumatic history.[2]

London Township: George Loveless's home at Siloam.
Photo: JJ Talman Regional Collection, University of Western Ontario.

The land of the London Township, as with other townships in Canada, had been divided up by the colonial government on a grid system, into units known as 'Concessions', to be rented to would-be tenant settlers who, as and when they were able to afford it, could purchase the land outright. In 1847, George Loveless purchased 100 acres of land (South ½, Lot 11, Concession XII) just west of Bryanston and 9 miles north of London Town. Now, for the first time in his life, he was a landowner! In 1852, George and Elizabeth sold up, and purchased a 100 acre farm (including homestead) from their son Robert (South ½, Lot 10, Concession IX), 6 miles north of London.

In 1855, George and Elizabeth's daughter Louisa (born 1839) died - an event which necessitated the creation, by her father, of the Siloam cemetery, situated just east of Fanshawe, there being no burial ground in the vicinity.[3]

By 1856, George had moved for the last time, having purchased a 48 acre farm (subsequently 50 acres, ½ of Lot 11, Concession V), also at Siloam. Here, on Fanshawe Road, he built a log-dwelling. He also built himself a rocking chair![4]

True to form, here, in London, George Loveless continued where he had left off in Dorsetshire as a Methodist lay preacher; walking miles on a Sunday, to preside over meetings and divine service, and utilising his most treasured possession, the *Holy Bible*, which he had purchased from Joseph Walton, convict of Van Diemen's Land.

A Methodist meeting house had been established in London, Ontario in the 1830s. It was served by a group of itinerant preachers, one of whom was The Reverend Stoney. Later, two Methodist churches would be built in the London Township: North Street and St James's. In 1857, George Loveless, with Anthony Metcalf (from whom he had bought the Lot 11 Concession V farm) and twelve other neighbours, founded Siloam's first (Methodist) church. Here:

> ...he sang and prayed, and often preached, for he was a gifted lay preacher and his services were given freely to assemblies whenever and wherever they were required.[5]

> Almost to the last, he held a Class Meeting [taken by a class leader for the purpose of counsel or religious instruction] on Sunday mornings.[6]

George's devotion to duty was legendary. Also his courage and selflessness, as is evidenced by this episode, quoted by author Harry Brooks:

George Loveless Junior. Photo: JJ Talman Regional Collection, University of Western Ontario.

A Mr Dickie, who as a boy knew George Loveless well, tells how when the whole of his (Dickie's) family had diphtheria, and his half-sister had died of it, the local minister was so scared of infection that he would not come near them and even shied of conducting the funeral service. His father appealed to old Mr Loveless [whereupon] he promised in a minute – he wasn't afraid to help a family in distress.[7]

In fact, George carried the lifeless body to the grave at Siloam and, 'probably performed all the burial duties alone as well.'[8]

When George's wife Elizabeth, died on 9 March 1868, aged 68, George continued to live on the farm at Siloam with his bachelor son Thomas, in the house which he had built on Fanshawe Road. George died on 6 May 1874, aged 77.[9] The couple are buried together, in Siloam's cemetery, beneath a single marble stone, in a plot adjacent to that of Martyr Thomas Standfield and his wife Dianne ('Dinniah' on her tombstone). In his will, George left his farm concessions to his sons George junior, Robert, and Thomas. (Both George and Robert married and became farmers. George and Elizabeth's two daughters have already been mentioned: Louisa, who died in 1855, and Sina, who died in 1844, on the voyage to Canada.)

A bridge spanning Oxbow Creek, to the west of the London Township is named after the Loveless family. Unlike the bridges in the Martyrs' native county of Dorsetshire, on which had been placed plaques bearing the inscription:

ANY PERSON WILFULY INJURING
ANY PART OF THIS COUNTY BRIDGE
WILL BE GUILTY OF FELONY AND
UPON CONVICTION LIABLE TO BE
TRANSPORTED FOR LIFE
BY THE COURT

The plaque on the London Township bridge was inscribed with the words:

LOVELESS BRIDGE
TOWNSHIP OF LOBO

GEORGE W LOVELESS 1797-1874
THOMAS A LOVELESS 1829-1912 [George's son]

(Beneath which were written the names of the London Township's Councillors).

Martyr James Loveless, younger brother of George, who had come to Canada with his wife Sarah and their three children, chose not to farm. Instead, in the London Township, he obtained a position as 'roadmaster' (a

157

post of civic responsibility, connected with the maintenance of the state of the roads).[10] He also became sexton (caretaker) of the North Street Wesleyan Church (opened 1854).[11]

After the death of his wife Sarah (the date of which is unknown as the North Street Methodist Church and its records were destroyed by fire in 1895), James remarried in 1849 to Ann Dagg, who, in 1853, bore him a daughter Emily (II).[12] James died in February 1873. He was originally buried at London's old Wesleyan Methodist Cemetery in Rectory Street. However, when shortly afterwards, the cemetery was sold for industrial use, James's remains were removed to the new Mount Pleasant Cemetery (opened in 1874) and re-interred there in an unmarked grave (Plot 264-B). His widow Ann, died in 1879, and is buried in the same location. In plot 263-B lies the body of Sarah Loveless, possibly James's first wife.[13]

Martyr James Brine was accompanied to Canada by his wife Elizabeth and their three daughters; also by his brother Joseph, and Joseph's wife Charity (daughter of Martyr Thomas and Dinniah Standfield). For reasons best known to himself, when he emigrated to Canada, Brine brought a blunderbuss with him. Perhaps he feared being ambushed by bush rangers, such as he may have encountered in Australia?

Initially, the Brines did not join their four Martyr companions, but instead travelled by ox-team to Huron County, 50 miles north of London. Here, they rented a farm at Homesville, not far from the shores of Lake Huron, and subsequently at Bayfield.

They went on to have 8 more children. Later, the Brine family moved to London Township to be nearer to the Lovelesses; renting a ½ share of Lot 14, Concession V1. Finally, in about 1864, they purchased a farm 20 miles north of London Town, in Blanshard Township near St Mary's in Perth County, where they built a homestead.

James Brine was converted to Methodism during the Methodist revival (renewal) led by James Caughey (Irish-born American who was ordained as an elder in the Methodist Church in 1836, and became a revivalist preacher in Britain, the USA, and Canada). For many years James was a class leader in the Methodist Church.[14] He died in 1902 at the age of 90 years. His obituary, printed in the *St Mary's Journal,* stated that he was, 'a devout and consistent member of the Methodist Church....'[15]   James's wife

Elizabeth, died in 1906, having also reached the age of 90. Both are buried in Perth County's St Mary's Cemetery beneath a single headstone which bears the words 'A member of the Tolpuddle Martyrs'.

In 1846, John Standfield purchased a farm in the London Township (North ½, Lot 10, Concession X), near to the hamlet of Bryanston. Here, he built a homestead and named it 'Dorset Hall'. When John vacated Dorset Hall in about 1858, his father Thomas, Thomas's wife Dianne, and their son John continued to live there. Meanwhile, John purchased two more farms just to the west of Dorset Hall (South ½, Lot 12, Concession XI, and North ½, Lot 12, Concession X). He now built another homestead: this time for himself, his wife Elizabeth, and their three daughters. John later moved to Bryanston, where he became a merchant in possession of a sizeable store. In July 1863, he became Bryanston's first postmaster.[16] John is credited with being the founder of the Bryanston Choir at which he and his father, Martyr Thomas, both sang. Thomas died in 1864, and his widow Dianne in 1865. As already mentioned, they are buried in the Siloam Cemetery in a plot adjacent to that of George and Elizabeth Loveless.

John, finally, moved to East London, where he became Chief Magistrate of the municipality - a complete role reversal from his Tolpuddle days. How times had changed! He also became its mayor, and the proprietor of a hotel.[17] Here, in Canada, he and his wife Elizabeth had four more children: Wesley (born 1848); Herbert (1850); Evangeline (1853); Gertrude (1855). Elizabeth Standfield died in 1883. John lived on until 1898. They are buried in London's Mount Pleasant Cemetery.

Robert Loveless (born 1800), brother of George and James, came to Canada in 1850.[18] He went to Stratford where, according to the *Stratford Beacon* of 26 September 1856, he formed a partnership, and erected a steam-driven wood planing mill. In 1858, he relocated to London where he purchased a part-interest in his brother George's farm. He later left the farm and purchased a grain and feed store in the town. Robert's wife Sarah died in 1868. He lived on until 1883.

Did the five men of Tolpuddle who had elected to emigrate to Canada,

James Hammett.
Photo: Trades Union Congress.

participate in any trade union activities in their new country of adoption? The answer appears to be no. In any event, they were now no longer landless agricultural labourers, but leaseholders of their farms. Nonetheless, for those who did take it upon themselves to challenge the powers-that-be, a harsh fate awaited them; for Canada was a British colony, under British jurisdiction. In fact, only five years before the Loveless brothers and James Brine's arrival in that country, forty-four, so-called, patriots had been tried for having been involved in the Rebellion of 1837-38. This was when William Lyon Mackenzie, the liberal Reform Party leader, became leader of a group which attacked what it perceived as the upper class ruling 'Family Compact' which controlled the government. Of these, all but one was found guilty: twenty-one were deported to the United States; six were hanged; sixteen were transported to Van Diemen's Land - the very place to which George Loveless himself had been transported in 1834.[19]

Martyr James Hammett, the only one of the six men who chose not to emigrate, was by 1841, living in his home village of Tolpuddle with his wife Harriett and their son George. Harriet bore him another four children. Now, James found employment, not as an agricultural labourer as before, but as a bricklayer. According to Mrs Mary Hammett, his niece, when James returned from Australia, he lived for a time in the cottage next to hers on the Dorchester side of the village (i.e. in Church Hill).[20]

Harriett died in 1860. James remarried again in 1862, to Charlotte, who bore him two children. Charlotte died in 1870. In 1875, James was married, for a third time, to Ann (née Frampton). She died in 1877. In old age, James went blind and, 'not to be a burden to his people [family],' he insisted on going into the Dorchester workhouse, where he was treated with every kindness possible.[21] He died there in 1891.

1.Brooks, Harry. *Six Heroes in Chains*, p.42, and Anderson, Geoffrey R. *The Martyrs of Tolpuddle, Settlers in Canada*, p.14.

2.*The Farmers' Sun*, 1921, in Anderson, Geoffrey R, *The Martyrs of Tolpuddle, Settlers in Canada*, p.14.

3.Anderson, Geoffrey R. *The Martyrs of Tolpuddle, Settlers in Canada*, p.26.

4.There is a difference of opinion as to whether George Loveless's last home was at Concession V or Concession IV. UWO photograph of George Loveless's final home gives its location as being on Concession V, as does an article in *The London Free Press*, dated 4 March 1952. However, *'Our Fourth Concession'* by Clarke E Leverette suggests by implication, and perhaps erroneously, that the Loveless home was at Concession IV.

5.Dr Fred Landon. Talk given to CBC Network. Reported in *The London Free Press*, 28 May 1954.

6. Brooks, Harry. *Six Heroes in Chains*, p.43.

7. Ibid, p.43.

8. Leverette, Clarke E. *Our Fourth Concession*. 1969. London, Canada: the Northridge-Stoneybrook Community Association.

9. Anderson, Geoffrey R, op.cit., p.21.

10. London Township: Minutes for 1846.

11. *The London Daily Advertiser*, 17 February 1873.

12.Anderson, Geoffrey R, op.cit., p.26.

13.Information supplied by London Public Library, London, Ontario.

14. Reverend JT Waddy. *The Tolpuddle Martyrs*, in *Methodist Recorder*, Winter Number, 1907.

15. Anderson, Geoffrey R, op.cit., pp.36-8.

16. Ibid, pp.33-35.

17. *The London Free Press*, 31 March 1951.

18. Anderson, Geoffrey R, op.cit., p.28.

19. Information supplied by London Public Library, Ontario, Canada.

20.*Memorandum of Interview*, 27 January 1934, Warwick University Modern Record Centre, Mss. JW/EG/612.

21. Brooks, Harry, op.cit., p.38.

Epilogue

From the day of his arrest on 24 February 1834, it is clear that George Loveless had no idea he and his companions had committed a crime (or felony, as it was called in those days). When the Magistrates' Caution was posted up in Tolpuddle on 21 February 1834, Loveless declared, 'This was the first time that I [had] heard of any law being in existence to forbid such societies.' At his subsequent trial, Loveless, when asked by Judge Williams if he had anything to say, replied, 'My Lord, if we have violated any law, it was not done intentionally....'[1] Trade Unions were springing up all over the country, and his would merely be one of many. Not only that, but three of his brothers: John, William and Robert were already, in all probability, members of trade unions.

Tolpuddle, The Green, Manor House, and Martyrs' Tree. Photo: Audrey Wirdnam.

On 12 September 1834, Loveless, now a prisoner in Van Diemen's Land, maintained the same stance when interrogated by its governor, George Arthur. 'I had no idea whatever, that I was violating any law...,' said he. 'I cannot see how a man can break a law before he knows that such a law is in existence.'[2] In this, Loveless received support from an unlikely source - a member of the establishment, namely the Home Secretary Lord John Russell, who, in a letter to Prime Minister Lord Melbourne dated October 1835, made the following statement in regard to the trial:

> Loveless gave a very fair, and I believe, true account that the evidence against him was agreeable to [i.e. was in accordance with] the fact, but that he took what he did from the suggestion of others, and that he did not know it was unlawful.[3]

Throughout all his tribulations, George Loveless held his head high; spoke the truth; attended to his work in a dignified and conscientious manner, and with his natural command of language and gift of eloquence, was quite prepared to debate matters pertaining to religion, morality, and of course, his beloved Tolpuddle union, with anyone who chose to question him on these matters. However, at a farewell benefit to the Martyrs, organised by the London Dorchester Committee on 8 October 1839, he finally lost his composure. Overcome by the warmth of his reception by an admiring, enthusiastic and above all, sympathetic public, he could contain his feelings no longer, and broke down in, 'a flood of tears.'[4]

And what of the Methodist Church which George Loveless had so espoused? Keith Salt, Methodist Circuit Property Secretary, writing in 1978 to a Mr Kent of Broadmayne, expresses regret at its inactivity in regard to the Martyrs.

> Methodism can scarcely be proud of its failure either to support the Martyrs, or to honour them, but the Church made some amends when, in 1912, a memorial Arch in front of the present chapel (built 1861) was unveiled....[5]

Sadly the Martyrs did not live to see it!

Author Harry Brooks, writing in 1929, quoted what an anonymous person who remembered George Loveless in Canada, had told him about the latter:

Of his love of the beauty of nature there can be no doubt. His flower garden was the delight and envy of all who saw it. His grandson, Tom [son of George II and Annie, née McGuffin, born 1863] tells of his grandfather's displeasure if anyone took a flower. He [George I] would say, 'You mustn't purloin one, but I will give you a hundred.'[6]

James Hammett was the only one of the six Tolpuddle Martyrs who chose to return home, permanently, after transportation. When he died in 1891, the indications are that his family would have preferred it if he had been buried in the grounds of Tolpuddle's new Methodist Church - built in 1861. However, the Hammett family was unable to produce a deed of agreement in order to substantiate its claim that a promise to this effect had been made to them.[7]

As for Tolpuddle's Wesleyan chapel, it eventually fell into disrepair. However, a new chapel was built by brothers William and John Hammett, kinsmen of Martyr James Hammett, which opened on 1 January 1863.

One may imagine George Loveless in his declining years, sitting in his rocking chair in the garden of his home at Siloam, admiring his garden flowers, savouring their aroma as it was wafted across to him on the summer breeze; sparing the occasional thought, perhaps, for Tolpuddle and his companion James Hammett, who had chosen to remain there after their return from transportation. Few could imagine, he declared, what experience alone could teach:

George Loveless's rocking chair.
Photo: London Public Library, London, Ontario, Canada.

What it is to be bereaved of, and torn from, those who are dear to us; and who are still dearer to me than could possibly be all the treasures of the world – Wife and children.[8]

George Loveless had truly been a much maligned man. However, now, with his beloved and faithful wife Elizabeth ('Betsy') at his side, he could rejoice in the fact that he and his four remaining Martyr companions and their children and grandchildren, were making a success of their lives in their adoptive country. Now, he could rest content, in the knowledge that he had lived that true, Christian life, 'stripped of the appendages and mystifications of priestcraft' which, he hoped, would, 'rise above all opposition,' and would, 'go down with revolving ages, enlightening the faith, enlivening the hope, enlarging the charity, enkindling the love, upholding the zeal; and directing the conduct of men, until the end of time.'[9]

On his and Betsy's shared tombstone at Siloam are inscribed these appropriate and moving words from the *Holy Bible's* book of *Revelation*:

> These are they which came
> Out of great tribulation,
> And have washed their robes,
> And made them white
> In the blood of the lamb.[10]

1. Loveless, George. *The Victims of Whiggery*, pp.7,9.
2. Ibid, p.14.
3. Quoted in Citrine, Walter (Editor). *The Book of the Martyrs of Tolpuddle, 1834-1934*. London, p.45.
4. *Cleave's Penny Gazette*, 19 October 1839.
5. Dorset History Centre, NM2:S19/MI1/3.
6. Brooks, Harry. *Six Heroes in Chains*, p.43.
7. Reverend E Benson Perkins, Department for Chapel Affairs, Methodist Church, Manchester, 7 July 1944 to JE Gilbert of Dorchester. Dorset History Centre, NM2S19/TS/2.
8. Loveless, George, op.cit., p.19.
9. Loveless, George. *The Church Shown Up*, p.16.
10. *Holy Bible*, book of *Revelation*, 7:14.

Appendix

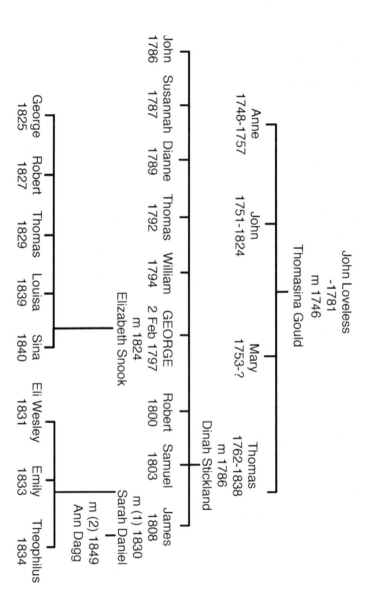

LOVELESS FAMILY TREE
(Surviving relatives)

John Loveless
-1781
m 1746
Thomasina Gould

Anne
1748-1757

John
1751-1824

Mary
1753-?

Thomas
1762-1838
m 1786
Dinah Stickland

John
1786

Susannah
1787

Dianne
1789

Thomas
1792

William
1794

GEORGE
2 Feb 1797
m 1824
Elizabeth Snook

Robert
1800

Samuel
1803

James
1808
m (1) 1830
Sarah Daniel
m (2) 1849
Ann Dagg

George
1825

Robert
1827

Thomas
1829

Louisa
1839

Sina
1840

Eli Wesley
1831

Emily
1833

Theophilus
1834

Bibliography

Dorset History Society:

Tolpuddle Christenings, 1718-1882. PE/TOL, RE 1/1-2 and RE 2/1.

Tolpuddle Marriages, 1754-1985. PE/TOL, RE3/1-4.

Tolpuddle Burials, 1813-1968. PE/TOL RE 4/1.

Anderson, Geoffrey R. 2002. *The Martyrs of Tolpuddle, Settlers in Canada.*

Biggs, Barry J. 1987. *The Wesleys and the Early Dorset Methodists.* Shaftesbury, UK: Blackmore Press.

Bridgeman, Major RO (Governor). 25 June 1932. *Historical Notes on Dorchester Prison.*

Brigden, Roy. 2003. *Ploughs and Ploughing.* Princes Risborough, UK: Shire Publications Ltd.

Brooks, Harry. 1929. *Six Heroes in Chains.* Poole: J Looker Ltd.

Buckler Gale, Elizabeth. 1983. *Farmers, Fishermen, and Flax Spinners.* Bridport, Dorset: Elizabeth Gale.

Census for Dorset, 1841 and 1851.

Citrine, Walter (Editor). 1934. *The Book of the Martyrs of Tolpuddle.* London: The Trades Union Congress General Council.

Citrine, Walter (Editor). 1934. *The Story of the Tolpuddle Martyrs: Centenary Commemoration.* London: Trades Union Congress General Council.

Dorset County Express.

Firth, Marjorie, and Arthur W. Hopkinson. 1934. *The Tolpuddle Martyrs.* London: Martin Hopkinson Ltd.

Frampton Papers, The British Library.

Gale, Elizabeth Buckler. 1983. *Farmers, Fishermen, and Flax Spinners.* Bridport, UK: Elizabeth Gale.

Hansard Parliamentary Debates. London: HMSO.

Hardy, Thomas. 1883. *The Dorsetshire Labourer.* Guernsey, UK: Toucan Press.

Hutchins, Reverend John. 1774. *The History and Antiquities of the County of Dorset.* Wakefield, Yorkshire, UK: EP Publishing in collaboration with The Dorset County Library.

Hutchins, Reverend John. 1774. *The History and Antiquities of the County of Dorset*, Edition 2, 1813, London: Gough and Nichols.

Lill, Diana. 1993. *The Tolpuddle Martyrs' Methodist Chapel.*

London Dispatch.

Loveless, George. 1837. *The Victims of Whiggery*. London, UK: Central Dorchester Committee.

Loveless, George. 1838. *The Church Shown Up*. London: TUC

Marlow, Joyce. 1972. *The Tolpuddle Martyrs*. London: Andre Deutsch.

Mee, Arthur. 1959. *The King's England: Dorset*. London: Hodder & Stoughton Ltd.

Methodist Recorder and General Christian Chronicle (1861 – present time). Ed. J.B. Watson. London: Wesleyan Methodist Newspaper Co. Ltd.

Padden, Graham (Compiler). 1997. *Tolpuddle: An Historical Account through the eyes of George Loveless*. London: Trades Union Congress.

Pioneer, The.

Putman, Bill. 2000. *The Romans*. Stanbridge, Wimborne, UK: The Dovecote Press.

Sherborne, Dorchester, and Taunton Journal.

Simon, John S. 1870. *Methodism in Dorset*. Weymouth, UK: James Sherren.

Tolpuddle Martyrs' Memorial Trust.

Tolpuddle Martyrs, The. 1838. *The Horrors of Transportation*. London: TUC Tolpuddle Martyrs' Memorial Trust.

Vicars, John A. 2000. *A Dictionary of Methodism in Britain and Ireland*. Peterborough, UK: Epworth Press.

Walker, W. Maitland. 1934. *An Impartial Appreciation of the Tolpuddle Martyrs*, in *Proceedings of the Dorset Natural History and Archaeological Society*, vol. LV, 1934. Dorchester: Friary Press.

Weekly True Sun, The.

Wesley, John. 1987. *The Journal of John Wesley*. Oxford: Oxford University Press.

Wirdnam, Audrey. 1989. *Pidela: an Account of the Village of Tolpuddle from Early Times*. Tolpuddle: Beechcote Press

Index

171

George Loveless, the only photograph in existence.